When We Talk,
Let's *Really* Talk

Empowering Begins at Home

One Story, Three Perspectives

Manisha Gupta, Naveli Garg, and Nitya Garg

When We Talk, Let's Really Talk

Copyright © 2022 by Manisha Gupta, Naveli Garg, and Nitya Garg

RHG Media Productions
25495 Southwick Drive #103
Hayward, CA 94544.

ISBN 979-8-9867434-0-0 (paperback)
ISBN 979-8-9867434-7-9 (hardcover)

Visit us on line at www.YourPurposeDrivenPractice.com
Printed in the United States of America.

What People are Saying

The everyday slices of life blend beautifully with introspective insights by the three authors."– Madhura Das Gupta, CEO, Aspire For Her

"Invites to reflect on what is a 'real talk' with many epiphanic moments. A book for parents and educators." Sophie Roumeas, Therapist & Coach

"As a college student, building my circle of trust with open communication will stick with me" - Shivani Amin, Nursing Student

"A reminder to communicate with loved ones authentically." - Rani Vakharia, High School Student

"*Unique in the literary world.* Difficult conversations, heart-racing emotions, masterfully documented". – Shamshudin (Sam) Kherani, Chief Dental Officer

"Every reader will walk away with *something special.*"- Poonam Rana, Technology Director

"A gutsy compilation of deep thoughts, the book qualifies as a breezy read on the surface but, in hindsight, makes one introspect deeper into the dynamics they share within their families." - Deepti Agrawal, Renowned Artist

"*It is a fascinating and relatable read that inspires us* to ask friends and family who they are and what they seek." - Julia Harriet, Author

"The book felt courageous, vulnerable, and honest - showing how to love and forgive by learning from one another." - Tiffani Jean Freckleton, RN.

"Consistent effort to engage, communicate, and understand one another in a family unit is time well spent." - MacKenzie Nelson, Author

"This book is beautifully written and will inspire and lead you to have more fulfilled connection and communication with your children. A gift to all parents" - Maureen Ryan Blake, Media Productions

"Provides realistic insights into how a family can intentionally cultivate a resiliently thriving future by developing inter-generational co-creative leadership!" - Dr. Kasthuri Henry, PhD. CEO, KasHenry Inc

"Being six is hard."
—Nitya, the night before her sixth birthday

"We are born to spend good time with each other and then we die."
—Naveli, nine years old

"With tenacity, we thrive together."
—Manisha

Dear Shalu Didi,

With a knack for finding sunshine through thunderstorms and clouds,
Ethereal, an epitome of giving, hiding behind innocent smiles.

Like spectators, we watch Stockholm Syndrome decay homes,
Adorn sufferings like gold petals,
Drip, drip you melt away, until one day you were gone

It's hard to forget you, giving even when you are gone,
Your story shines forever,
Empowering conversations in homes.

- With lots of love from lots of us.

Love to

Gunjan (Dad)
for being our anchor and supporting us in his unique ways.

Our Circle of Trust
friends and family members for everything they do for us.

Zoey and Zion
for choosing us as their family.

Contents

Our Families Shape Us

This book may be read as one about psychology, family, team, leadership, or individual growth.

According to Johns Hopkins Medical Research, an estimated 26% of Americans age eighteen and older suffer from a diagnosable mental disorder yearly. In addition, one in twenty-five Americans lives with a severe mental illness such as schizophrenia, bipolar disorder, depression, anxiety, and eating disorders. Mental health disorders are snowballing across all countries. Yet, they remain widely under-reported, creating an economic problem as a social one. The phenomenon is not just in the USA. Rather, it is worldwide.

A nurturing family environment can play an instrumental role in addressing this challenge. As the tiny neurons create and connect, the feeling of belonging and the reassuring confidence to be heard goes a long way in strengthening emotional resilience.

Through a series of conversations, three individuals experiencing life differently bring to light the role families play in nurturing wholesome individuals and, hence, societal well-being. We are a mother-daughters trio who bond over tangible projects and philosophical conversations. Through the day, we oscillate in our individual journeys, searching for our questions and their answers. Then, as the night falls, we lean in on each other to broaden our perspectives or sometimes just to feel heard as we prepare to venture into the world the next day.

The pandemic was changing everything rapidly. While we waited to preview the future, the similarity in the news circulating on TV, corporations, universities, and schools became apparent. Within days, the jambalaya of topics had tilted from natural catastrophe to mental health, anxiety, substance misuse, insomnia, depression, and more. Young kids and adults alike were impacted across the world.

We, too, had started experiencing the weight of loneliness locked up inside our rooms, often glued to our screens. Debates flared up between the openness of our commute-free evenings and the opacity of our disturbed minds. Arguments morphed into discussions. And as we connected, we felt lighter, not alone anymore. Humans are feeling objects that think. We are happier when we feel connected. Heard. Seen. We thrive when we are free to be ourselves - becoming ourselves, being a journey of action, reflections, and adaptation.

Unfortunately, our modern lifestyle makes this a rather challenging endeavor in the cacophony of voices, biases, and expectations. Fortunately, within the confinement of our home resides the perfect antidote. Family values are emphasized across cultures, yet this ancestral awareness is lost in our fast and furious race for progress. Families like teams can mold us to become thriving individuals or disturbed beings. We, too, as a family had experienced both ends - the good and the bad. As we became conscious of the influence we had on each other's life, we tried to create only a positive difference. Practice improved our chances of success.

The subtlety of experience was in intentionality, which makes us aware of ourselves and of others. However, when driven by reactive compulsions of today's lifestyle, we tend to either take each other for granted or simply ignore them. This realization was quite unsettling.

Then, as we shared our stories with friends and colleagues, they sparked conversations for them, reconnecting them with their families. Stories were instrumental in rekindling close ties. More importantly, stories had a commonality across families.

In December of 2021, we caught the bug and were confined inside our respective rooms to quarantine. But we continued our discussions, only this time over Facetime and Google Docs. Writing was cathartic and made conversations clearer. Through it all ignited the idea to co-write this book to capture topics that often surface in conversations across age and life stages.

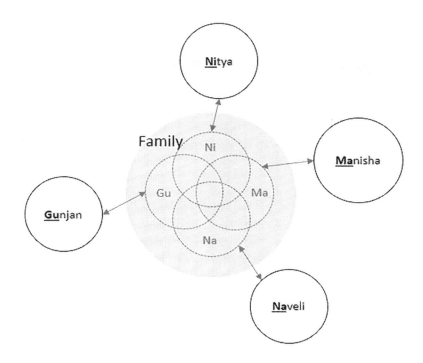

Our circle of trust starts with our family unit and extends to close friends and extended family members. Yours may be different. We hope that by sharing our stories or trials and tribulations of candid conversations with each other, we have fostered the idea of investing in building your circle of trust. And then indulge in genuine conversations - talking freely and listening intently without judgment. Because once we try and experience the benefits of candid discussions, we want to try more. Each step we take toward each other makes us feel more wholesome.

Gratitude,
NaNiGuMa

Characters

As independent thinkers growing up in a single-family unit, open, honest, and constructive conversations kept us connected. Our perspectives were often different. They taught us to listen to make others feel comfortable in sharing candidly. Our differences made us conscious of not judging each other when our thoughts refused to align. We also learned to agree to disagree.

Our conversations are often impromptu, though some are structured and intentional. We share a few conversations we had with each other through this book, monologues through which we remunerate our individual perspectives, and reflections we captured in our personal diaries.

Nitya

Look out the window to a bright blue sky,
Who am I? A butterfly, I fly
Flying by dance, debate, bio all in the blink of an eye.
Yet I still get tongue-tied.
I shoot high.
Thereby,
Sometimes I lose battles.
I cry, wave good-bye, but then I apply…
Applying these learnings to my everyday life
My family aids me,
I have become a Swiss knife.
Hoping to be happy, and proud
Of the person I become
When we meet in the afterlife.
~Nitya

I am currently a high schooler exploring subjects, learning life lessons, and discussing with my family to understand who I want to be and what I want to do. My natural curiosity often drives me to question topics ranging from meditation to medication. My artistic traits have pushed me to immerse myself in dance, singing, and arts. At the same time, my methodical mind juxtaposes me to pursue business, finance, and debate. Along my journey to explore the world's knowledge, I find myself perplexed by social situations and moral dilemmas. With the guidance of my family, I aim to learn and become my best, happiest, and most accomplished self. An individual I can be proud of and happy to be.

Naveli

Lost and confused, I have stood
Contemplating life at times too early to tell
Sometimes alone, sometimes together
Words withholding the weight; don't bother
I define myself as strong and clear
But my purpose and definition have wavered
I define myself as uncertain with direction
But that life is okay. I concede
I, a woman, an Indian, an adult, an American
I, a student, a teacher, a leader, a dancer
I, a friend, a sister, a daughter, a child
I, in pursuit of connections forever
Lost and confused, I have stood
Needing the guidance and comfort
That words, I have found,
Can ever tell
~Naveli

I am Naveli Garg, a fourth-year Psychology with a Biological Emphasis Major, double minoring in Dance, and Gender, Sexuality, and Women

Studies (GSWS). All my life, I have witnessed connections and disconnect between family members, friends, and generations alike. I have also experienced that harmony can be created with different opinions and voices. Voices like my own, my parents, my sister, my friends. In my family, each member has strong beliefs. At times stimulating, other times opinionated; at times stupid, and other times intellectual conversations in my household pushed me to become open sometimes and difficult other times. We grew together and finessed our voices along the way. In pursuit of open and honest conversations throughout my life, I write this book. Our differences can only make us stronger.

Manisha

I am a mother, a wife, a daughter, and friend,
A dreamer, a learner, a student, and employee,
An achiever, a stability factor, a technologist, and business mind,
An Indian, an American, a traveler, an explorer,
An author, a reader, a painter, a hiker,
A heart, a hand, a body, a soul,
All within.
I am all that and perhaps more,
Yet often, I stand alone.
Oscillating between these roles,
Like a pendulum,
From numbness to restlessness.
Sometimes lucky to find the center,
Fondly I call it wholesomeness.
I am strong and weak,
Privileged and deprived.
Accomplished and invisible,
Bonded and free
It all depends on where you stand
And what you see.

Noisy waves come in all forms -
Society,
Family,
Work,
And creations of my own.
Some surface me up,
Others topple me down
The world expands and shrinks,
And sets forth choices
To compete, judge, and confine
Or care, trust, and set free.
~Manisha

Society flourishes when families nurture wholesome individuals, and their environment lets them be. Wholesome, for me, is a feeling. The freedom we earn through an arduous process of discovery and doing. A process intertwined with that of others as we oscillate from one role to another. This book reflects upon my daughters' many roles in my life as I have played in theirs. The only difference between us, in the end, is just age, experience, and our roles.

Na-Ni-Gu-Ma

Our journey started with CharityDress, a social venture to "do what we could" and help those less privileged. CharityDress connected people from all walks of life while providing clothes, education, food, and broader perspectives. Then, during the pandemic, we launched "Conversations with Art," a YouTube channel to stir dining table conversations on topics light and heavy through the universal language of arts. When secluded from the outside noise during the pandemic and locked in the same house, we debated our evolving perspectives from school, college, and professional lives, which evolved into this book.

Time is the currency of relations, and a story is the most effective communication method. Words are so simple. Yet so complex. We sincerely hope our stories will spark meaningful conversations and deepen connections between you and your loved ones. And as you start talking, we hope this book reminds you to talk freely - share candidly, listen intently, and value perspectives over judgment.

Continue the conversation at www.NaviNiti.com.

Clarity

Which candle am I?

Trampoline

Family - a unit that centers us through the ups and downs of our individual journeys.

Nitya

Allowing one specific number to hold multiple meanings seems absurd. We have infinite numbers to choose from, yet we use the same number to address the emergency line (when we desperately need help) and, ironically, the famous coordinated terrorist attack that shook Americans; **911**. What's more fascinating is that everyone unanimously accepts the two uses as mutually exclusive. Literally everyone.

Before 1968, when the go-to telephone number became 911, and before 2001 when the attack occurred, the numbers 9 and 11 held no significant value. The same can be said to be true for many others. In the past, the numbers 3 and 13 may have represented a biblical verse, a card game variation of Rummy, a 2014 drama, the Badri Battalion military unit in the Taliban, or even perhaps the angel number representing happiness. But after 2020 and the pandemic, it means March 13th, the day on which schools were shut down nationwide.

Naive and unknowing, I came home excited for a "two-week" vacation; or so I had wrongly understood then. After a rocky freshman year, more socially than academically, a short gap sounded just perfect. However, by the time I had bitten halfway through the break, and the following Monday, March 23rd had dawned upon us, more cases had spread worldwide. With every passing day, it became more apparent that this would be more than just a "two-week" break.

Despite spending a delightful week – slacking, cooped up in my room, endless FaceTime with friends, and living oblivious to the reality of the situation, I had reached the heights of boredom towards the end of my ignorant but blissful week. So, I leaped onto my old-time favorite, sitting serenely in our backyard, a thick blue rim around a bouncy black bed - our very own trampoline. It was just as majestic and robust as I had remembered it, ready to bear my weight in its fourteen-feet-wide lap.

I have noticed that most houses have that one thing - a gadget, a room, a prized possession that its owners become overly accustomed to. Yet, it continues to awe everybody that visits the house. In our home, it was our trampoline.

One summer in elementary school, Didi (what I call my older sister) and I had worked hard to read book after book to complete the grandpa-inspired one hundred book challenge; the prize was going to be a trampoline. Mom's love for beaches had inspired her to make a sand bed on which our gardener had assembled the trampoline. We used to love playing in our enlarged sandpit, jumping onto a chair, climbing on our trampoline, and then reaching for the ripe persimmon growing at the tip-top of the tree. It used to feel like a dream to do that in our own backyard in those days. However, coming back home and lying there seemed routine nine years later - except for today. Today, as my back pushed against the recoiling springs, uncertainty seemed inevitable.

Naveli

It was March 7th, 2020. The beginning of the end of my second quarter at UC Davis. The headline *New Campus Directives for UC Davis* hovered prominently on my silver MacBook screen. The administration had made a last-minute decision for our next week's finals to be online instead of in person. Internships and events had been canceled. The coming spring quarter instruction was up-in-the-air. And with no explicit direction for the next two weeks, if not more, I sat with my dorm roommates – Fatima and Catherine – contemplating what each of us would do.

Classic college wooden bunk-bed structures surrounded us. A bike stood next to Fatima's desk. In front of me was a color-coordinated weekly schedule that had all our classes for the quarter marked. It had only been six months of college. Six months of exploring and figuring out who I was and who I wanted to become. For me, the concept of freedom had begun to thicken. So, the question was, now what?

Uncertainty lingered in the air. It was throughout our dorm floor. Yet, many were somehow ecstatic, treating it as an extended holiday with no end. But for me, someone who was just getting a footing in Davis, spring quarter was supposed to be when I immersed myself in college. Planning to rush pre-professional Greek life, I thought I would perhaps find my tribe and understand myself better. Taking academic courses that interested me, like biology, got me excited. Labs, social life, and clubs that were all supposed to help me discover life but were now at a halt. While the first two quarters at Davis had been riddled with low self-esteem, confusion, and a wavering social life, this next quarter I had designed to *save* me. But instead, it was *failing* me, and it hadn't even started.

Being from the Bay Area, home was only a short hour and a half drive. Beyond making it easy for me to visit home during freshman year, the short distance also became a major deciding factor in where I would live for the upcoming quarter. Home seemed like a better place to navigate the uncertainty of the next quarter. By March 15th, UC Davis officially announced that our spring quarter would be online. And the same day, it was confirmed that I would be moving back home after my winter quarterfinals.

By March 17th afternoon, Catherine had moved her belongings out of the room, and I followed suit. My mom and sister came to pick me up from Davis that evening. As I ran around my room, packing everything up, I hesitated. I had barely been able to talk to my friends; everything was ever changing just a bit too quickly. Within a few hours, my entire life at Davis was packed, hastily stuffed into the back of our Audi Q7.

That drive back home was memorable, to say the least. Parked at a random gas station in the middle of the city of Benicia, I broke down.

Confused, Nitya asked, "What's wrong?"

"I have no idea... I guess I didn't say good-bye. It ended too early. I didn't get the full experience..." I said brokenly.

I didn't understand my emotions about the next quarter. All I know is that I felt overwhelmingly uncertain, like the earth under me was shaking.

Thinking about all of this, I walked downstairs late on March 23rd afternoon. It was spring break, but it didn't feel like it. Without any official end to the holiday, the thrills of break diminished. I had therefore slept in, not excited about the days off but anxious about my future.

Turning the electric kettle on, I saw Nitya lying on the trampoline, basking in the mid-March sun. From elementary school through to high school, we would occasionally nap on the gigantic trampoline outside. A thing we hadn't done in a while. Nostalgia settled in. And it was just too tempting to resist.

Climbing onto our now-broken patio chair, I looked at her, who invited me to join.

Manisha

I scanned my calendar to find my next meeting was at 1:00 p.m. I had an hour free in the middle of the day. *What a blessing*, I thought as I prepared to grab a cup of water.

The walk from my home office to our kitchen was short. As the water trickled into the cup, I glanced at the kids settled comfortably on the trampoline. Faint giggles and occasional acrobatic gestures were visible through the corner of my eye.

The kitchen counter was messy; someone had left the crumbs from their croissant on its shiny granite top. The sink had dirty dishes, and the backyard door had been left open, allowing for a mildly cold breeze to delicately balance the sun rays peeking through the clouds.

The product, People Analytics, which we had worked on for three years, was scheduled to launch in August. I had nurtured this product like a startup, anticipating the market moves and customer needs in a fast-evolving industry. Unfortunately, we also had to wade through immense internal pressures. While Financial Analytics were well understood, the value of People Analytics was often questioned.

We had a vision - to enable employers and employees to thrive together. Unfortunately, organizational biases often impede leaders from knowing the absolute truth, leading to the untimely death of high potential products and people. A problem I aspired to solve as Analytics evolved. And so, we toiled. My go-getter team took every challenge in stride - each person unique like a finely chiseled Lego piece, bonded together with trust and respect. Our motto - to anticipate a problem before it becomes one - motivated us and partners both internal and external.

Paid customers are the best antidote for all doubts and resistance. Early customer sentiment was positive, and we were eager to close the first customer. However, as we prepared for a crucial demo with the customer executives, the onboarding team reported an issue. An oversight, a bug uncaught in internal environments, became glaringly visible in the customer's pod. People Analytics would only work if the customers had bought Financial Analytics.

Unfortunately, the customer neither had nor intended to buy Financials, so we were stuck. And a pesky bug now had the power to create false perceptions with customers and Oracle decision-makers. The meeting had been planned a month back, and rescheduling would push us out by a month or more. With a week to go for the demo, we brainstormed a creative solution to avoid this disaster.

We set up a fake financial account for them. Though the experience was clunky, People Analytics now worked on their pods. We also knew they cared deeply about their concern about the pandemic. So, we scrapped daily updates on cases offered by Worldometer to build custom extensions to analyze the impact of the pandemic on their global offices.

About a week back on the demo day, the customer team noted the clunky workaround. We apologized and then redirected their attention to the custom extension and closed the demo with, "The product bugs will be fixed, but the architecture will help you navigate unknown challenges like the pandemic." The CHRO chuckled, complemented, and confirmed her decision to buy. We closed our first deal months before the official launch. *One down, two more to go*, I had thought.

A week had passed since the office closure. It was 12:12 p.m., Monday, March 23rd, per my phone. Mondays are usually commotion-filled in our home as the weekend fades into the chaos of weekday mornings. Today was different. Stagnant. No walk. No chirping of the birds. No commute. No coffee. No breakfast. No break, just a laptop. I was still in my pajamas.

Today I had also woken up to an email, "Congratulations on the win. We would like to prepone the launch to May and make this a tier one launch. Your product evidently sells well." Evidently, the sales rep on the call shared the story with her manager, which reached the Oracle executive team within minutes. What followed that email was a series of meetings from various groups within Oracle. Today was that day.

Like the dark gray sky indicated the rain ahead, the morning meetings had set the stage for the chaos ahead. Months had to shrink into weeks, days would become longer, and pressures higher. And we would have to do all this remotely over Zoom.

The sight of the girls on the trampoline was a welcome break from the monotony of the rushed launch. Naveli lying on her back, Nitya on her stomach. I took a sip. As the cold water trickled through my dry throat, I grabbed a croissant and ventured out to join them.

Trampoline

"How are my girls doing?" I broke the ice.

"Not sure; there's just too much uncertainty," Naveli said aloud.

"I am sort of happy that I can attend school in my pajamas," Nitya chuckled.

I climbed up beside them. "Remember we used to talk here often when you were younger?" and reflected loudly, "Feels good to be back on the trampoline."

"We used to sleep here too," Naveli added.

"And listen to Mom's random stories," Nitya commented with her lips pressed on the blue synthetic sheet.

"Do you want to hear a story?" I asked them.

"We have grown up now. But sure." Naveli signaled me to narrate, and both closed their eyes.

I started narrating.

"Feel this.

"You are a candle in a box full of candles sitting on a shelf in a super-market. One Sunday morning, a little girl comes with her dad to buy three candles for her birthday cake. The shopkeeper picks up four candles - pink, purple, yellow, and white. He lights up the white one next to the idol of his God near the cash register and hands the other three to the little girl's dad.

"At home, the father decorates the candles on the birthday cake. As they light up the yellow candle, the doorbell rings, and more guests come in. They hug and kiss in excitement and forget about the burning candle. Unfortunately, by the time they come back to the cake, the yellow candle is already halfway burnt. So, the dad hurriedly lit up the other two candles and moved the cake to the kitchen island so the guests could stand around it.

"Visible through the island is the kitchen window, and through that window is visible a nearby mountain. Hikers were trying to climb the mountain. Birds and animals were scattered, some gazing at the grass, some resting."

"Like Mount Diablo from our home," Nitya chimed in.

"Right. Like Mt Diablo," I continued.

"The purple candle peeked out of the window as the guests assembled around. It was getting dark. The purple candle, now inspired, wanted to glow at the top of the mountain to light up the hikers' path. Its prayers were answered when the girl blew quickly, smothering its flame, picking it off like a weed, and putting it on the side of the table. Ignoring the sickening feeling of the spit, the purple candle pulled in all its might, attempting to stay alive. But unfortunately, that lit up a spark from the tiny fire still simmering in its wick. The dad noticed the flame and waved his hand so vigorously that the candle fell.

"Mom noticed the remaining two candles - yellow and pink, still sitting on the island. The yellow candle was almost finished and went straight into the trash. She cleaned the pink candle and put it inside the little girl's memorabilia box, to bring back fond memories for when she was older.

"Meanwhile, a little boy kicked the purple candle lying on the floor. The candle took its chances and started rolling. It rolled out of the room towards the roadway, through the front door, and on the road. It rolled and rolled and rolled until it reached the foothill and then continued rolling up the hill. It reached the midpoint on the hill after years of cruising. Tired and somewhat broken. Self-doubt creeps in as it falls asleep, wondering if it was still bright enough for the hill.

"By the morning, it regained strength and conviction reappeared. And it started rolling again. The wind threatened to blow it away as it neared the top. Determined, it hid under a rock to block the wind, until the wind gave up. Just as the purple candle plans to roll again, the rain strikes. The thunderstorm warns her – 'survive, then thrive.' The candle obeys and rolls back under a shrub. A few days later, the rain too gives up, and the candle starts rolling again.

"The summit day arrives, and the purple candle is now at the very top of the hill. The view unblocked for a tiny flame to light up the mountain. The candle now eagerly waits for the sun to set and the hikers to arrive, so it could show them the way.

"But the journey wasn't yet over. Out comes the afternoon sun red in anger and growls, 'The top is mine and only mine. My scorching rays shall melt you. Stay here and die or roll back and live.'"

I paused.

"So then?" Nitya opened one eye, raising her eyebrow.

"So the question is - what will you do? And which candle are you?" I asked.

"Okay, Mom, you always cook up stories to make us see things." Naveli swayed her head smiling and added, "Which one are you?"

But before we could continue, Nitya got up. "Enough talking," she said as she sprung up to jump and pulled us up with her.

Nitya's Diary

Once Didi and Mom's weight had joined mine in rediscovering our home on the trampoline, the bittersweet feeling of uncomfortable uncertainty paired with comfort of togetherness pepped us all. We all came individually, dealing with our own emotions, yet we all sat together, hoping to bounce back.

And as we lay there in the glaring wave of the swindling summer afternoon, we surveyed the once-ripe-now-bitten persimmons on the persimmon tree.

"Everything is going to be okay," I thought.

North Pole

Stay focused and stay open.

Naveli

After spending a few moments with Mom and Nits that day, I felt lighter. Yes, there was uncertainty, but I had to stay focused on my purpose - my North Pole. Was I overlooking the passage itself in my impatience to earn the rite of passage? "*The journey had to be cherished as much as the destination.*" Mom's words rang in my ears.

We have all read the uberly-interesting coming-of-age books. From the deep philosophical ones such as *To Kill a Mockingbird to* elementary classics like *Anne of Green Gables* to newer dystopian-era ones like *The Giver,* coming-of-age books often became a makeshift guiding path. Kids from Hidden Hills Elementary School synonymized "growing up" with the journeys portrayed in those books. For me, there was a fascination – or perhaps romanticization – with growing up. Freedom to be who you are. An expression you create. An identity that solely is yours. Built up by a community surrounding you, supporting you. Imaginably a crucial one, guidance didn't register to be of importance. Not until much later.

By fourth grade, a staple series arose in my life: The *Harry Potter* series. Though I displayed no knowledge of magic, the twists and turns of finding one's true self were intriguing. Of being a hero. Of being on the right path. Of hope and light and everything in between.

Mom used to sit down with me then. It was ritualistic... school, extracurricular, home, then homework. Math Olympiad on Saturday. Bharatnatyam on Sunday morning. Balvihar on Sunday afternoon. After-school soccer became piano lessons, which became different dance classes. Margie, Nupoor, repeat. "Family Fridays" were weekly planned occurrences, resulting in game nights, movie marathons, or dinners. I was in elementary school, and life felt pretty all right.

A routine in place, I used to sit on my white Ikea desk and finish my homework before the scheduled "downtime." The primary attribute was that I finished work on time with the help of a stable work ethic, one instilled by my mom. Weekly, sometimes daily, we would sit at our wooden circular dining table, going over all the deadlines for that week. Slowly and steadily, the concept of deadlines sank in. Mom had the reins, guiding me through elementary school and its learnings. The occasional late-night poster board runs occurred much more infrequently than my peers.

I graduated fifth grade and grew aware of the twists that middle school would bring. With a new chapter in my academic life came new rules in my personal life. Growing up meant Mom was around, but I was to take charge now. The onus was 100% on me to meet deadlines and deliver quality work. My life's direction was solely in my hands.

Friendships changed, and I found myself academically on top of things. First-semester sixth grade brought its own perils; somehow, it was easy enough to sail through. By the second semester of sixth grade, I became more confident in my abilities and cockier. Thinking I could finish a mini project in an hour, I procrastinated. And procrastinated some more, until I didn't have enough time to finish it. When my teacher asked for my project, I didn't have it. And I got my first *ZAP*.

Zeros Aren't Permitted – ZAP, in short – was a Windemere Ranch Middle School program where students made up homework for partial credit. A late policy of sorts, assignments that fell under that category needed to be turned in a few days after the deadline unless you willingly accepted a zero in the grade book.

That night, I came home, faced with the challenge of breaking the news to my parents. I was supposed to be on top of things. But I wasn't. I had never missed a deadline. Yet, I just did. And though the assignment would still be accepted, there was still a penalty for late work. It just felt like a disaster.

Mom and I sat on my bunk beds purple and white bed sheets – our spot where we had many deep conversations. My white lamp wall-shelf was turned on. Next to me was my pink and black "One Direction: Where We Are: Our Band, Our Story" poster.

"Mumma... I did something bad." I looked at the "Whether You Can or You Can't, You're Always Right" poster hung across from me on the wall of my lilac room. Gaining a bit of courage, I said, "I didn't submit an assignment and got a ZAP," pulling the white, half-page ZAP slip from my pink backpack.

"What happened?"

I answered, everything sounding a bit like an excuse. Finally, I caved. "I procrastinated, Mumma. I don't know why."

Mumma put her hand on my thigh. Staring into my eyes, she said, "Find your North Pole, Navi."

"What? What's a North Pole again?"

"What do you want to do in life? Or this year? For anything that you choose, you need a guiding direction. Your North Pole helps you achieve whatever you ultimately want to do."

I was confused. "How does my North Pole affect me right now?"

"It's not about the destination, Navi. It's about the journey. At any point in time, your North Pole is the next step that you need to take to eventually reach your destination, your dreams. It's very difficult to just sit and think about what you like. When you start doing something though, it becomes easier to know if you like it or you don't."

She continued, "Like you know you like to dance after you have danced. You know you didn't like soccer after you had played some. For certain things it's also better to learn from others until we draw clarity. For example, there is some wisdom in pursuing basic education. So, for now, your North Pole is to finish this assignment and stay on top of other deadlines."

Something clicked. I understood a bit more about what I needed to do. Since then, we have had several discussions on the North Pole, though the origin of my journey to find my North Pole is a moment I will never forget.

North Pole is a word that has been repeated to me at least a thousand times, if not more. A concept that I struggled to grasp. A mountain I still aspire to conquer as I continue my ever-perpetuating journey to find my North Pole and repeatedly lose track of it.

Thinking of the North Pole today mothered an urge to ask Mom about its origin. Out of an impulse I texted, "Guys, how about having lunch on the trampoline today?"

"Sure," replied Mom. "12:30 p.m. or 1:00 p.m. works."

"1:00 p.m.," Nitya confirmed.

On the Trampoline

"Mom, I was remembering the story of the North Pole today," I shared as we climbed up.

"North Star might have been a better choice of words, but perhaps my love for mountains deflected my words away to the North Pole," Mom commented.

"Well, it stuck, and hopefully, one day we will visit the actual North Pole," added Nitya

"Mom, you must have explained the concept a hundred times. Do you remember the first time we talked about it? In fact, what made you come up with that?" I asked.

Nits and I savored our sandwiches as she narrated her story.

"Growing up in India, we had rich community experiences. Unfortunately, though, our options were limited when it came to extracurriculars. We were only allowed to pursue activities available at school, and if lucky, learn from a teacher if one happened to live within our complex."

Mom paused to take a bite and then continued.

"I had been keen to learn swimming and guitar, but we neither had a pool nearby nor a guitar teacher. So, I spent my childhood pursuing arts - painting on my small notebook with watercolors or bonding with neighborhood kids over hide-and-seek and hopscotch games. Luckily Papa's frequent relocations offered rich exposure to a range of cities, schools, and friend circles. Also, being a voracious reader, Papa ensured our house was full of exciting books, my favorite being the *Why, Why, Why* and the *Famous Five* series. Every new experience expanded my passions and aspirations."

She paused as our eyes followed a bird flying over us.

"Your childhood was different. The US societal ecosystem is not the same as India's. But classes were accessible more easily. The global economy powered by technology has also made everything much more accessible. So, I was keen that you both get a rich exposure and have a good shot at living holistically."

We danced our eyebrows as we smiled.

Mom went on. "I don't know how much you remember now - the efforts we would make to try new things, explore new activities, and meet people from different walks of life. In fact, till date, I keep looking for opportunities to seek different experiences."

"Experience over stuff!" I chuckled.

"Thanks to Groupon and Expedia," Nitya chimed in.

Mom continued, "Right. So anyway, when Dad was in India, we spent our evenings after work and school in your elementary years exploring. I drove for you to dance a few steps on different tunes, swim a few laps, dribble, and kick different types of balls, immerse in all sorts of arts with brushes, hands, and everything in our garage. We petted animals of all shapes and sizes and tried everything we felt like trying that we could afford to try."

"So where did the North Pole concept come from?" I interrupted her.

"Well, choice also has a little sister named confusion. It was important that you understood the dichotomy between opening options when seeking exposure and converging when it was time to seek closure. So, as you prepared to enter middle school, we indulged in a conversation."

Mom was now looking at me. "It was a conversation about Napoleon. Does it ring a bell?" Mom asked.

"Vaguely," I responded.

"Napoleon Bonaparte, the French military general, the first emperor of France?" Nitya asked.

"Indeed. A powerful king who used to craft very detailed war plans, which he hardly followed. Any guesses why?" Mom asked.

"Maybe he wanted to try something new?" Nitya chimed in.

"Or maybe his original plans didn't work," I added.

"Yes. I read that Napoleon was swift at adapting as he learned about the enemy's plan, the climate changed, or food shortages happened, or his soldiers fell sick." Mom continued, "So why did he keep making very detailed plans still?"

Mom continued, "Edward Tufte, a political science professor at Yale and a pioneer in data visualization, talks about Minard's seventeen-dimensional chart of Napoleon's 1812 march in Russia accounting for terrain, climate, army size, direction, food ration, etc., etc."

I gulped down the last bite of my sandwich and signaled that she had answered her own question.

"A thought-through plan made him feel in control to start with. Then as he moved a step closer to the enemy, he learnt new things and adapted his plan accordingly," Mom shared.

Then Nitya asked, "And if there was no new information?"

"Well, then he might have stuck to his original plan or adapted if he came up with a better plan with previous information," I chimed in to answer this time.

Nitya then slid in the moral of the story, "When we have a plan, a North Pole, we are never lost. "

"But we have to be open to learning more and flexible to adapt as we learn more," Mom was quick to add.

"So, make a plan, my North Pole to stay focused or let's say not get swayed away all the time with distractions. And, as I learn more about myself and my options, adapt the plan. But give me enough time to try out my original plan before changing. Otherwise, I might not reach anywhere - neither the North Pole, nor the South Pole!" I internalized aloud.

"Maybe you will reach the equator!" Nitya was good at not letting the opportunity pass.

"Too hot there," I winked as I continued to ask Mom, "Okay, so that was the story it all started with. What happened then? Did we work on a project after that? Did you make me work on something? I mean, I think I feel like I have heard about the North Pole a lot by now."

Nitya nodded.

Mom smiled, "No, it was you for this one. Over the next few days, you had asked me tons of questions about the North Pole – 'Do you have a North Pole? Isn't Santa from the North Pole?, "How often does your North Pole change?, What if I don't know what my North Pole is? or What if I want to change it'

"That summer, we drafted your North Pole for the upcoming school year as you prepared to experience middle school. We also created a commitment rule of one year. We would stick to the plan we finalized for the school year. As we learn new things, we will adapt the plan next summer. Your North Pole for the sixth grade was new friends, studies, dance, and public speaking."

"So, basically, try to visualize your goal. If you have the end goal in mind, it's easier to reach there by working backward," Nitya clarified.

"Yes, it is about being intentional, not as much as about any specific goal. For example, we may decide our North Pole is to relax and do nothing for the long weekend. Or you may decide to take a gap year before college. An intentional gap year vs a gap because you were too lost and too late to apply are very different types of breaks. *One instills confidence and the other takes it away*," Mom clarified further.

"Navi, for example, in the tenth grade you liked computers, and so in the eleventh grade, you signed up for Java and the innovation and engineering class. As you went through the classes that year, although you liked them, you were not as excited about them as you were with women studies, biology, and in understanding the human brain. So even though at the end of eleventh, you signed up for advanced engineering, post our long discussion during the summer, you applied to switch to biological sciences instead."

"Yes," I agreed.

"Did you feel lost or in control each year?" Mom asked.

"In control at the beginning and maybe lost towards the end of the school year," I replied.

"Fair enough. You adapted your North Pole based on your new learnings that year. We can only *commit to taking one step at a time, but after taking the step, we can pause to evaluate if the previously defined path is still the best option or if we want to course correct*." Mom offered more examples.

"Got it, Intentional. Take charge." Nitya in Nitya's style, jumped up. "Time to get back to school in pajamas again."

"Stay focused on the step when you are taking it, but open in between steps so you can course correct if need be," was my conclusion.

We glanced at the phone, now showing 1:29 p.m. It was time to head back to our rooms.

Nitya

Since elementary school, I've heard Mom and Didi talk about this "North Pole." I never knew exactly what it was, but I assumed it was a symbolic north star: a solid guiding light. While this wasn't often a direct conversation I was a part of, the message was quite clear: it's good to explore once you know where you're going, once you know your "North Pole."

My North Pole was to get good at whatever it was that I was pursuing-which meant high grades. The first understanding of why we get an education was learning in order to insure a bright and stable future. But at one point, this phenomenon started making less and less sense. I wondered, *Why do we study from elementary through high school for sixteen years of our life... just to study more?*

We hear that getting accepted into top colleges like Ivy and UCs is an assurance of a prosperous future. But what does that even look like? How do we measure success in the real world? The education system makes success seem much like a pursuit of who can make the most money, but I believed it was about becoming the best and happiest version of myself.

In fact, when we think about why the system is the way it is, the end product makes no sense. Adults pitched the educational system to empower the next generation. But there are far too many faults and gaps for this attempt to be sincere. First, my school used to start at 7:32 a.m., expecting us to sleep early and wake up early, even though Laura Sterni, an MD doctor at Johns Hopkins explains that teen bodies are proven to have a far harder time sleeping until after 11:00 p.m. Next, some colleges only look at GPAs and SAT/ACT scores to determine acceptance, even though research by William C. Hiss has proven a limited correlation between those scores and future "success." Even colleges that have finally adapted to go test-blind just turn to another type of test score, the AP tests.

The epiphany that school isn't really serving us, that it's outdated, and that it doesn't factor in the nocturnal reality of its students depolarized my North Pole. My sense of security in what I was doing escaped, and so did my confidence in the concept of a North Pole. So how do I know what I want to do, where I want to go, who I want to become... if the system meant to help me succeed doesn't add up.

I debated and tried hard to visualize what real success could look like. The more I retaliated, the more lost I felt. I think that's when I may have finally understood the importance of having a direction, whether it's called the North Pole or something else. When I felt like I had nowhere to go, I felt purposeless. Those who wander may not always be lost but wandering aimlessly for too long does start giving you a feeling of being lost. After a while, we want to feel back in control. At least, I thought I did.

There's this game we play in the car. One person picks a number and another the direction to turn many times, and then you just drive. It was fun for a while, but finally, we decided where we *really* wanted to go. Our final North Pole. Similarly, navigating high school or even college hallways without a plan felt like fun for some time, though, in the end, it made me feel lost. Too many new ideas and no clear direction added to my confusion more than building my confidence.

But what I didn't know until Didi was applying is that I can take baby steps. All I have to do is decide my North Pole *for now - the first* step I need to take. And it's okay; in fact, it is encouraged to adapt as things become more evident. After all, hopefully, I will only turn wiser with time. So, for example, I can start college undecided. Not knowing precisely what I want to do in the end does not mean I have lost my North Pole; it just means I am more open to finding it the right way. And although the system may not be perfect, and I may not exactly know what I want to do in the future, having some direction gives me a head start.

So as of today, I see my North Pole. I see myself prioritizing my future - holding my academics to a certain regard as well as expecting a certain level of performance in my extracurriculars. I demand myself to meet most deadlines and know when it's okay to take a break. I expect myself to study finance and marketing in a decent, tiered school. I expect to prioritize a balance between social fun and work. And I expect myself to have some sort of financial literacy when spending. These are all the things I prioritize today, right now as I write these words on my MacBook Air keys and Grammarly's squiggles signal me to actively edit my thoughts. But tomorrow my North Pole might change, and that's something I am more than comfortable with.

Naveli's Diary

The dichotomy of staying focused while staying open is hard to grasp. We are all trying. Together.

Conviction

Be and let me be.

Blue People

Keep your curiosity and conviction alive.

Nitya

Finding a moment of availability among the three of us for the remainder of the week proved difficult. Even at a young age, academic homework and extracurricular started eating away at my free time. And with Mom and Didi being older, I always expected them to be even busier than I with work, and the academic rigor that comes with being in older grades. It was surprising how difficult it seemed to find a moment in common until the week came to an end. So finally, as Friday afternoon dawned upon us, we decided to take an extended break. My school ended at three, as usual. Mom moved her meetings to make time, and Didi's schedule was quite flexible, so our aligned schedules found light under the sun's warmth. A light breeze invited us to take an afternoon siesta on the trampoline - and we accepted.

On the Trampoline

I was in no mood to give in to my inner turmoil about school and grades. Instead, wanting to talk about something light, I asked the gang, "So, what are we going to talk about today?"

Mom and Didi looked at each other as if they had something in mind, smiled with their half-comical-half-mysterious smiles, and blurted out together, "The Blue People."

"I asked for it, didn't I?" I played along. "All right then, what about the Blue People?"

"Remember how mad you were for being brown?" Mom's eyes were twinkling, ready to tease me.

"Yes, we have heard that story many times. Let's do an improv-style act out today just for fun. You and I played by us, and Didi can be that nice lady."

"Sure, in any case, the nice blue people were called Navis." Didi reminded us of the resemblance to her name "Navi" and jumped on to land right next to me.

Blue People

I set the stage.

"James Cameron's *Avatar* was breaking all box office records as the media raved about its jaw-dropping visuals, excellent use of 3-D, and the immersive setting of Pandora. A hybrid human-alien called an *Avatar* facilitates human communication with the alien planet's indigenous Na' vis, *who had an unconventional blue skin color.*"

Mom added, "We all watched the talked-about movie screening in the neighborhood movie hall on a Friday evening. The demand was high, and our planning was last minute, so all the good seats were taken. We settled ourselves in the fourth row from the screen, uncomfortable with our necks tilted yet satisfied to be able to watch it still. Nitya, then four, sat in my lap. The science fiction heightened her curiosity. As the scenes rolled, so did Nitya's whispers with comment-like questions. Sometimes the question would become louder, and I would hush her to be silent, pointing her towards the other folks sitting around us."

"All right then the scene begins," I nudged them to get into character.

"Nitya, hush. They will be disturbed," Mom whispered.

I nodded in consent and continued my commentary. "At this point in the movie, we were eager to watch the preparations for the inevitable fight between the brown humans and the blue Navis."

We carried on with our play acting and after a brief pause, I whispered again, "Will they fight?"

"I think so," Mom whispered back.

"I don't like brown people."

"Hmm," Mom acknowledged.

"They are hurting the blue people."

"Hmm," Mom nodded.

"Mom, who is from Earth?" I whispered again.

"The brown people," Mom replied in whispers with her eyes intently glued to the sky (our pretend movie screen).

"Wait. We are the brown people," I now shouted back, sounding upset.

"Shhhhhhhh. Not so loud," Mom was now following a bird flying over.

"But I want to be the blue person. I don't like brown people." I pretended to be angry.

"Hushhh," Mom repeated.

She then set the stage for Didi's entry. "I had started to feel a bit embarrassed when we heard laughter, and then a comment from a lady sitting a few seats to my right. "

"Sweetheart, not all brown people are bad. You are the good one." Didi, acting as that nice lady, suggested.

Startled yet satisfied by the comment, I, reacting as my then four-year-old, bundled close to Mom and stayed silent for the next few minutes as we stepped back from the act into the current.

A couple of minutes later, I spoke up again, "Mom, what happened then?"

She narrated matter-of-fact, covering her eye with her hand to avoid the sun. "As the movie ended and the lights turned back on, we received smiles from many of the folks sitting around us. A few struck a dialogue with you about the movie and comforted you that you were indeed a *good person even with brown skin.*"

The breeze was light and the sun bright. We all lay there for a few silent moments together.

Mom was the one to break the silence. "I learned something that day. As our family thanked the people for their understanding, I noticed that strangers had nurtured Nitya's curiosity when I was squashing it out of embarrassment. Then I started thinking about shame - when and why do we start hushing our curiosities away."

"So, what did you learn?" I asked.

Mom got up and went inside the house, signaling us to wait. She walked back with a diary in hand and settled back on the trampoline. This time she was sitting up with our heads close to her lap. She turned a few pages and started reading -

Manisha's Diary

December 25, 2009

The magical blue people are everywhere, if only we pause to look.

What do you see when watching a child not yet influenced by the plethora of societal dos and don'ts?

I see a mind full of curiosity, a heart full of innocence, a head held high without fear, a flame burning with a desire to explore the world around them. I see raw, fresh, and pure life as aspirations, craziness, creativity, and happiness. I see the truth. And I see the dare.

I cherish their curious questions - why do plants not have eyes, but potatoes and dogs do? I relish the lessons they self-acquire when the teacup feels too hot to the bare skin, and the breath not held underwater makes them lose their balance. I love watching with them as the coffee and the wine sweep through the carpet to see which one leaves a deeper stain. I find comfort in cuddling through tears, unhappy with their skin color. They ask anything, try everything, laugh their hearts out, cry their guts out, get lost in the activity engaging them, and learn to navigate and create.

We cite stories about child resilience, children coming from different lifestyles, and making life-changing discoveries. They embrace the magic within and create magic outside. They trust their instincts without seeking their brains' approval. Instead, allow the brain the time it needs to catch up through logical proofs and debates. They are unbound.

Some people stay unbound even past childhood. Whether they choose to be a cook, a dancer, a hiker, a creator, a baker, an artisan, astronaut, whatever they do, they try to do a little more. We meet such enviable human spirits lazing on a sunny beach joyously, contemplating the surfboard's angle to hit the waves. Geniuses like Picasso, Monet, Beethoven, and A.R. Rahman immersed so profoundly in their art that they became the art themselves. Such dreamers' dream of capturing the sun, and inventors trap the sunlight to light up our nights. Some make us travel across oceans, and others want to take us to the moon.

What do you see when watching such an adult?

I see a mind full of curiosity, a heart not so innocent, yet a head held high without fear, a flame burning with a desire to explore the world around them. I see raw, fresh, and pure life as aspirations, craziness, creativity, and happiness. I see their truth. And I see their dare.

I see them honing in on the magic within them. And I see their magic making our lives magical.

The magical blue person is also inside me if only I pause to look. It's up to me to let it live. For me. And for those I love.

Back on Trampoline

She closed her diary and lay down again beside us. I think she was still reflecting on shame, or maybe magic, or both when she started speaking again, in spurts as she remembered things -

"You know I love traveling, especially to non-touristy places.

"While walking through the villages and the countryside in India, Japan, Africa, Mexico, Nepal, Sweden, London, Canada, and even the US, I witnessed creativity and innovation buzzing in most households.

"I saw half-cut inverted Coke bottles used as funnels, old clothes tied to trees to create swings for children, bamboo sticks repurposed as knives, and shoes made from worn-out car tires.

"Their homes display a unique collection of things assembled as rooftops to seek protection from the sun and the rain. Everything was acceptable for home construction, from used polythene bags, grass, twigs, and broken pipes. It seems as if ..."

"As life keeps throwing new challenges at them, these innovation hubs respond with new solutions - within budget, within time, and with the high quality required to sustain such harsh life."

"Hmmm." It was my time to respond in syllables.

Mom continued, "After a couple of days of exploring these streets, I always find myself expecting to see more creations that are ingenious. However, the initial feeling of surprise alienates me in an ecosystem that wires everyone to explore what's possible, all the time."

Mom was silent now.

Then Didi picked up the conversation, "Remember Dharavi?"

She continued without waiting for us to respond -

"During our visits to Dharavi, the biggest slum in Southeast Asia, we found elementary school children using ice cream sticks, bottle caps, and cheap solar panels to create light."

"Hmmm," I added with my eyes still closed under the afternoon sun. I was enjoying this rhythm now.

Didi continued, "They were eager to build mobile apps and solar-powered streetlights to address molestation, which is frequently happening on late nights in those dark streets. It was so much work, yet so much fun helping them build those solar cars and assembling the light demo."

As if they were participating in a relay race, she passed the baton back to Mom, who shared another of her travel stories.

"During my travels to Rwanda, I visited a family slated as level ten, the lowest in Rwanda's socioeconomic strata, we were told. This family of eight had one goat, a tiny home, and a small patch of land they could call their own. Their home was a small shed with a tin roof, mud walls covered with reused polythene, and one wall dedicated to memories: fading pictures, hand sketches, and emotional memorabilia adorning it.

"In front of that shed was a tiny, six feet by six feet mud puddle, one side covered with a heap of leaves and grass. The damp patch protected with an indigenous wooden fence made from local tree branches was the often-visited retreat for their goat.

"Adjacent to the shed was their patch of land, which grew wildflowers prevalent across Rwanda (no seed, water, or attention required) and carefully planted local veggies. They used every inch of everything that was growing. The local grass and the wildflower leaves fed the goat, and the goat milk fed the family kids.

"They offered us a tangy drink made by soaking the wildflowers in water in a single cup to be rotated and shared amongst all guests and family members, thereby neither requiring containers nor dishwashing detergent. The family beamed with pride as they walked us through their self-developed ecosystem, which helped them save enough *money to buy their goat.*"

"Quite creative. Can we now go back to how shame kills the magic within us, and we start shushing each other?" I came out of my hibernation to say a couple of words.

Didi, a psychology student, shared her perspective. "Mamma, your stories indicate that curiosity and creativity pervasively foster in a child's heart as in villages. Yet, something changes ..."

"What changes? And why?" I now had to catch up with two philosophers.

"Maybe in towns and cities where we can afford formal education, we transition from being a problem solver to a job seeker," Mom offered a perspective.

"Wait, are you saying schools destroy us?" I wondered if she finally understood my point about schools and grades.

"Perhaps the intensity of our needs diminishes as life becomes more comfortable, and we learn to tame the creative human brain towards a conforming societal machine. After all, necessity is the mother of creation, as is the crisis of innovation."

I could see Mom's eyes not wanting to make it easy for me, so I decided to go back to the comforting, "Hmmm."

"We are a Ferrari capable of zipping through the mysteries and the adventures that await. Yet as soon as we put one foot on the accelerator, we feel compelled to put the other on the brakes. Somehow, we learn to create self-imposed inertia and deprive ourselves of the magic within us. We do it so often that the magic dies for so many of us without getting a single opportunity to manifest itself. It is a shame what we do to ourselves in the process of growing up." Mom was staring straight at the afternoon sun.

I did not know how much I had understood yet. So, I clarified, "Are you saying that so much resides within us that it is difficult for us to comprehend?"

"And even if we explore freely, it takes many attempts to identify our magic," Didi added matter-of-factly.

"And even if we are trying to find that magic, our curiosity may sometimes be silenced with hushes and embarrassment from people around us," I confirmed. Then suggested, "But we can choose to be the Ferrari that zips through unknowns fearlessly."

"We will listen to societal dos and don'ts, respect everyone's opinions, yet fan our convictions." Didi, as usual, brought in the balancing angle.

"Can we add school dos and don'ts too? And yes, we will keep our curiosity and conviction alive to discover and play on our strengths." I was getting the picture.

"The irony is that all the hush stops once you succeed. Read the biographies of anyone who made a difference. They, too, were affected by external pressures. But their unwavering conviction helped them stay on track and bounce back. They lived to become their best selves and the best in the world." Mom was smooth in reminding us to stay focused.

The sun was now lower in the sky, and the breeze was getting a little chilly. "We started with a story on hush. Shall we close with one on "no hush?" I asked a few seconds later.

"Sure. Let's listen to the Christmas story, the cookies we baked for Santa!" Didi chirped like the bird on the persimmon tree.

No Hush

After a few minutes of silence, Mom went on to narrate again.

"Dad had left for India again. I had joined Deem, a startup, and my entire team focused on making the release on which our funding depended. So, days and nights were passing by, juggling work and kids.

"It was already Dec 24th. A year earlier than the *Avatar* movie. Our Christmas tree was still not set up. I went to work that morning, promising you both that we would set up the tree in the evening.

"We were engrossed in an intense design discussion for a problem with the release at work. Three of us were whiteboarding the solution in the war room when Alba, our nanny, called. Not wanting to disturb the discussion flow, I texted her, 'Can I call you later?' and continued the whiteboarding.

"While working through the demanding initiative's grueling hours, several of us had fostered deep friendships. We were well versed in each other's family situations. I remember Sai and Bhavna, my colleagues, signaling me with their eyebrows as if to ask, 'All well?' as I assured them with a nod that it was.

"My phone rang again.

"I texted again.

"It rang yet again.

"I picked it up and put it on the speaker while still focused on the whiteboard.

"'Mom, we have a situation.' I heard Nitya's voice and understood that Nitya had made Alba call me.

"'Is everyone okay? What happened?' I was paying only half my attention to the call still.

"'We have no tree, no milk, no cookies.' Naveli was anxious in her voice.

"'Hmmm,' I was listening.

"'How will Santa come?' Nitya's loud cry was perfectly timed within the few seconds of silence amidst the ongoing debates in the war room. The deep worry in her agitated voice became apparent to all my colleagues.

"'I am coming, Nitya. Give me some time.'"

"'Mom, can you not work tomorrow? Santa only comes on Christmas Eve.' I heard a melancholy appeal from Naveli now.

"Before I could answer, Sai did. 'Absolutely, that is important, Navi.'

"He then continued, 'Manisha, you need to go now. Prepare cookies for Santa and bring back some cookies for us too.'

"I scanned the room to see everyone smiling and whispering, 'Go,' as one added, 'We can handle this situation. You take care of the critical Santa situation.'

"My body was tired, and my brain occupied. The seventy-five-minute drive with loud music helped revive the energy, especially as I drove over my favorite San Mateo bridge. My team's gestures reminded me not to let fatigue or work squash your conviction that evening. I reached home around 5:00 p.m. when it was already dark outside. As I entered, your hugs and cheers lit up, at least the inside of the house.

"We assembled the tree and decorated it one ornament at a time. Significant measures were taken to ensure that the decorations were balanced throughout the tree. Not just on one side. We decided that the side facing the fireplace should have the best decorations. That was expected to be the side Santa would see first as he came from the chimney. Once the tree was done, our team moved on to bake a variety of cookies, and as the night fell, we laid out a tray with a glass of milk and a plate full of cookies to invite Santa to our home."

"The night was cold. I turned the fireplace and the TV on for you as I prepared dinner. It was going to be 'Quick Maggie' night. Expecting to see huge smiles as I walked back with bowls of Maggie, I was dismayed to see an expression of worry on your faces.

"'What's wrong?' I asked.

"'Mom, how will Santa come?' It was Naveli's turn to question.

"Before I could make up an answer to that question, Nitya added, 'You know Santa comes from the chimney. But we turned the fireplace on.'

"Suppressing my deep desire to laugh aloud, I nodded in concern. 'We can turn off the fireplace and take more blankets instead.'

"You two rushed to fetch the blankets as I switched off the fireplace.

"We ate Maggie and watched a movie. Then before hitting the bed, Nitya insisted that we open the fireplace and check if the chimney had cooled down. Thankfully it had, allowing us to sleep worry-free that night.

"We woke up to a half-empty glass, some half-eaten cookies, and gifts wrapped by the elves in shiny Christmassy wraps. Santa finally came, and all our efforts had paid off, making our day magical indeed!

"Tada. The end," Mom announced.

"We know who Santa that night was," Didi responded.

"So moral of the story is, no more hush." I got up, now feeling quite cold.

"Indeed, no more hush, but you are not kids anymore. So, as grown-ups, take ownership of keeping your curiosity and conviction alive." Mom winked.

"Really, Mom, we won't be talking about blue people next time we watch *Avatar*." I chuckled.

"We can, but this time to discover the magical blue person hidden inside you." She smiled.

"Hey, I feel like having Maggie," Didi announced.

"Sounds good. If you two are cooking." Mom smiled.

"Yes, we are the magical grown-ups now." I pretended to use the tree branch as a wand.

Manisha's Diary

It matters not how strait the gate,
    How charged with punishments the scroll,
I am the master of my fate,
    I am the captain of my soul.
-Invictus by William Ernest Henley

Nitya's Diary

Moms as in mothers
A soul helping the others
The light in bad weather

Whether we win
Whether we fail
Fail everyday
They're okay
Cuz they're there
And they're where
Where we need them be
They never flee
No matter if we beg or plea
An unspoken dut-ie
The duty of being a mom, my mom

Naveli's Dairy

Mother, Mother.
Written for Mother's Day in middle school.

Mother, Mother
I am here, I am here
Mother, Mother
Just stay right here
Mother, Mother
Don't leave me nowhere
Mother, Mother
I can't find you anywhere
Mother, Mother
I know where you are
Mother, Mother
You are here, not far
Mother, Mother
I found you now
Mother, Mother
I am happy wow

Mother, Mother
Are you here, are you here?
Daughter, daughter
With you right here,
Forever in your heart
as are you ever in mine.

Thrive Together

Accepting others requires accepting ourselves.

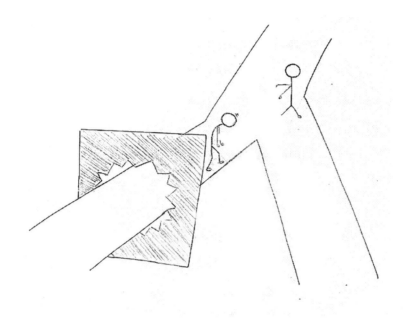

Naveli

The trampoline and the trivialities at home helped bounce back from the uncertainties. I had parked myself on the round table at the kitchen and family room intersection. Basking in the sun, which had entered through the glass backyard door.

Mom passed by, phone in hand and a cup of tea in another. Hearing her disconnect the call, I asked, "Mom, so which candle are you in your story?"

"All of them," she smiled, and walked away.

"All of them?" An unexpected answer. I wondered what Mom wanted to convey. Was each candle a chapter in her life? My life? Life had indeed started seeming like a bouquet of experiences. My pensive mood drifted me back into the past again.

Naveli's Diary

That day was vivid, like a Van Gogh painting behind my closed eyes.

As the emotional crowd gave a standing ovation, the dance piece on 'cyber-bullying' proved impactful. Amidst cozy hugs, my dance teacher announced, "Naveli — now that's a voice worth listening to!" My voice? Tears flowed down my unrestrained cheeks — tears the world understood as those of joy. I envisioned the situation differently as I flashed back to other unforgettable days.

On the way home from middle school on a desolate trail, a group of clearly inebriated high-school boys had accosted me out of nowhere. They mercilessly tore the clothes from my body as if I were a piece of meat. My kicks didn't save me. The forceful hand covering my mouth overpowered my feeble attempts at wiggling my way out of their grasp. With the last vestige of courage left in me, I bit on the hand covering my mouth. Finally, the grip loosened, and I ran my way back home. The contents of my backpack lay strewn across the trail; their laughter and shrieks rang in my ears. Ashamed and fearful, I left my clothes and trust in people behind.

I had lost my voice that day.

I felt responsible. Launched in a state of depression, I shut down. The only thing offering temporary solace was dance. Hence, I had started "Naveli time": thirty minutes locked in my bathroom, singing into my hairbrush, dancing my heart out. The intensity of my kicks broke the toilet seat twice. Slowly, painstakingly, the weight of the molestation lessened. My weak voice was at least a whisper now. I had believed all ugliness was behind me.

This belief was tested again as a rude shock strangled my voice in junior year. A friend had deceivingly intoxicated and assaulted me. Somehow worse, my perpetrator was my then-boyfriend's best friend. He then convinced my boyfriend that I had instigated the event — that I had cheated — turning me into the villain of their story.

A friend I thought I could trust and a boyfriend who was supposed to protect me turned on me as if I was a pest they needed to squash. Anticipating backlash, my perpetrator proceeded to belittle me over social media. Mean comments, texts, and gossip wrecked my social life. Victim blaming ensued. Friends lost to lies drove me to desolation. Pushed to close all my social media accounts and change my number, I isolated myself. A pariah, I became a shell of my former self.

As before, I had taken recourse in the arms of poetry and dance. After singing into my hairbrush during "Naveli time" for six months, I pulled myself together to take a stand and raise my voice against cyberbullying. Investing all my energy into the production, I worked tirelessly for five months. With the deafening applause from the audience, I knew I had made a difference.

As fate would have it, the story repeated yet again in college. Slaps from a friend stung my body and face. People say three is a pattern. I believed for a while that maybe I was the problem.

Escaping the relationship and through my friends' push, I consciously decided to rebound and not waste my life feeling victimized, blocking my own progress. So instead, I diverted my energy to study human behavior and address societal issues.

I feel like the purple candle in Mom's story. Maybe the story was to remind me that loneliness and leadership are related. But the one we focus on is the one who befriends us.

At the Round Table

It was evening. Mom and Nitya joined me at the round table for a snack.

"Things are uncertain. But I think I'm strong." I announced it to them and to myself.

Both smiled as Mom hugged me. "Uncertainty can be tiring. Character building. Yet sometimes, it can also misguide us, especially if we let anxiety and judgment take over us."

Nitya nodded. Then after a long enough pause reflected aloud, "At my high school, the mindset is hyper-fixated on our future. Something we know so little about. Yet, we are bred to contemplate every possible aspect of college, our career, and what we believe to be our entire life. All that at just sixteen. Little do we know that life is more profound than college's thin, shallow layer."

Mom and I were listening as she continued.

"We are under so much pressure, constantly judging ourselves for not doing enough. Unfortunately, we sometimes misplace that same judgment upon others. But why are we judging? Is it because we are so fixated on what we believe is a success - on college- landing in Stanford and IVYs and UCs? When success has so many faces. Honestly, I, too, have been subject to this."

I chimed in. "Nitya, maybe it is because we are copying each other's definition of success. Nothing wrong in aspiring to be in IVYs or UCs."

"Indeed, it's good to dream big. Try hard. But also let go if it doesn't work out. Use rejection as redirection. Something always works out in the end. Like you did, Navi." Mom was smiling at me.

Then in her mom-like manner, she moved on to Nitya. "Nitya is also bringing up a good point; why do we judge?" She paused, looking inquisitively at Nitya now.

Nitya's eyes were lost in the bluish-gray sky, contemplating.

"This girl with whom I had mutual friends in middle school. She was short with shoulder-length hair and wasn't seen as super-bright academically. After school, kids would walk across the street to the library to hang out and possibly do homework. Over a few such trips to the library with her, I realized how different her lifestyle was from mine. I had never realized what it meant to have divorced parents - especially for your academics. I had seen movies where parents worked together to co-parent, and the kids maintained bonds with each other. The movies don't show you that if you for-get something when you switch houses- let's say a textbook - you may not be able to get it back for a while. Even the liberty of time is snatched away. Your time and emotion are occupied with shifting houses and ensuring your parents' love doesn't fall through your grasp, cracks, and into their new family."

She looked at us. Reassured that we were with her as we nodded, she continued, "After that, I tried my best not to judge others. When people ask my opinion on someone, I would simply tell them I didn't know them well enough to judge them. While I couldn't always convince my friends to avoid these conversations, I decided I could avoid adding to the rumors and misconceptions."

I felt so proud of my little sister.

Mom noted, "Trust and love are the antidotes to fear. Lack of trust mothers fear. It increases stress hormones and makes it challenging to work together. Being able to trust the other person, on the other hand, nurtures a warm feeling toward each other. We feel like working together. We feel more creative. Heard. Understood. And thrive together as a family, at school, and at work."

Nitya then shared a marvelous experience she had had. "In high school, my school's leadership teacher, Mr. Bowen, introduced a program called *breaking down the walls*. Most kids at school weren't exactly sure what it was, and despite being in leadership, I wasn't either. We were told to expect something along the lines of group therapy. But it was so much more. I remember coming home and repeating Mr. Bowen's words to Mom - *it's harder to hate somebody once you know their story.*"

"Tell me more." I was now cozied up on the papasan next to the table.

Nitya obliged.

"The event started with ice breakers, encouraging us out of our comfort zones. Then, we were asked to participate in seemingly odd activities. Such as sharing personal things with strangers. As the day passed, the giant gym had begun feeling cozy.

"But perhaps the most impactful experience of the day was *the silent walks*. Everyone was asked to stand on the longer edge of the basketball gym floor in silence as the head adviser instructed, 'Take three steps if...' He had warned us that they would dive straight into some tough questions. I had no idea what to expect until he announced the first one, 'Take three steps if one of your parents has passed away.' Of the 120 students and staff, fifteen took a step. The ninety-nine questions that followed revealed glaring and daring life situations. Mental health, suicidal thoughts, academic issues, rape, family members in prison... After every instruction, he'd ask us to look around to our right and left and remember that these people share something in common with us. That day I discovered so much about myself and so many around me with whom I now empathize.

"There was also beauty in staff participation that day. As students, we often discount our teachers and administrators, unaware of their life situations. Some of them hide so well behind their reassuring smiles every single day. The last exercise of the day was to share the most challenging question we had to answer when a girl, perhaps a year younger than me, broke down. She then shared that although she couldn't recollect the last time her parents had expressed that they were proud of her, her coach did all the time. She confessed the exercise had made her realize how much her coach had done for her despite the coach's own struggles.

"I also observed how strong everyone was and how sometimes our seemingly small actions and words impact them. Unfortunately, we often start believing that the only way to shine our light is to steal the air from somebody else's flame. But, in that room, the 120 of us were proof that we could all *thrive if we were aware of ourselves and others.*"

Mom and I were listening intently. We all stayed quiet for a while, then Nitya concluded, "I also learned that my judgment came from a place of loneliness. And that accepting each other requires us to accept ourselves first. Then we can turn our differences into our collective strengths."

Manisha

We manifest trust through our willingness to be vulnerable and open with each other. And we do it if we believe the other person has good intentions towards us. Building trust takes effort within a family and in a professional setting. Still, it's worth the investment as it has a direct, positive, economic impact on team performance and social and economic growth. Maya Angelou aptly summarizes my learning, "I've learned that people will forget what you said, people will forget what you did, but people will never forget how you made them feel."

I have cycled through a few jobs and teams so far. As I join a new team, I work to strengthen the emotional trust within the group. Beyond the lunches, dinners, and drinks, we take personality assessments and share them to identify how we mirror and complement each other. Improv and team-building activities also help. My goal with this exercise is to increase trust and our collective sense of belonging. Profound emotional bonds also offer a higher sense of purpose, which generates feelings of happiness and productivity.

My favorite is an exercise I call the Circle of Trust. We try to plan dinners for this though sometimes have to do with lunch settings. Dinners have the extra advantage of drinks that help get the guards down. We sit around a table, preferably round. Each member then goes through the room and shares an area of strength and improvement for each person. The recipient is only allowed to nod or say 'thank you.' I always start the exercise with three reminders: a) We all create perceptions about ourselves through our behaviors. Take these inputs as the perceptions you might have made for the person sharing an observation. You can choose to use or lose the feedback as you deem fit. b) Feedback is a gift. It is easier for a person to stay silent and create water cooler rumors. Forming a circle of trust requires courage and intention. If possible, try to appreciate the courage shown today in sharing these perspectives. c) What happens in Vegas stays in Vegas. Emotions are invited today and constructive follow-ups encouraged. Temptations to retaliate or gossip are strongly discouraged as they breed toxicity in the teams. I also encourage the team to approach me with feedback about the process itself.

To break the ice, I often initiate the circle, and once the flow begins, most people join naturally. To cultivate trust, we have become trustworthy and trusting - I share my honest perspective with direct eye contact, speaking slowly and intentionally. Then I listen without interrupting as others take turns to vocalize their perceptions. Leading by example makes me confident and others comfortable in following suit.

There hasn't been a circle yet when people didn't feel emotional. At times there were tears. And once a person politely refused to participate, which I learned to accept. The days that follow are also charged with emotions and excitement. There is more laughter in the workplace. More lunch invites. Some constructive jokes become part of the team's vocabulary.

I am thankful for the occasional post-it notes that appear on my table and leave a lasting impact on me. The exercise helped one person understand that being honest with each other is an act of courage. Another person shared how she learned to provide constructive feedback by observing others. People also internalized that they can't expect the recipient to do things differently just by giving input as the post-it read, "I don't oblige by changing as soon as I receive feedback. It takes me time and sometimes clarifications." Another shared how he had wrongly created an opinion for a team member and how the exercise helped him understand his blind spots through others' complementary feedback on the same person.

Manisha's Diary

Demonstrating and cultivating trust is the most critical job for parents. A feeling of trust within family members helps kids develop emotional stability, confidence within themselves, and an awareness of others.

The building blocks of trust and distrust, an outcome of behaviors, start when we are young. So, the onus is on parents, teachers, and adults to work on and grow it for our kids by providing a collaborative environment to explore their own experiences through interactions with us. Naveli's unfortunate experiences have made her uncomfortable with last-minute shocking surprises from trusted people. Uncertainty has now become a trigger point, making her feel emotionally low, perhaps an eerie feeling of mistrust and fear for her. Nevertheless, it is good to see her owning her recovery through reflections and open conversations. She is finding her center again. I am happy for her and proud of her for wanting to find her way back home to her happiness.

Credibility

To thrive together, understand self, and others.

Open, honest conversations make it easy to reflect upon our own stories and behaviors. Often, we would share our narratives over evening walks. Each of us had unique experiences that encouraged us to go the extra mile. The commonality was that most impactful were the childhood experiences.

The Climb

No quitting - push through tough until it becomes easy.

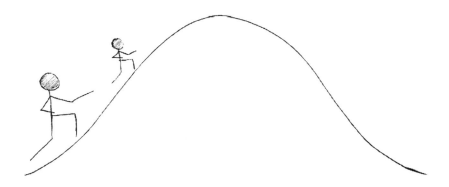

Naveli

Almost

"Whether you think you can or you can't, you're always right." -Henry Ford

While growing up, I heard this phrase so much that it almost became my catchphrase- reflecting on my studies, extracurricular, friendships, and family. I was a strong-headed child. If I wanted to do well in something, I would put my all into it. But, on the other hand, if I was relaxed and didn't make a conscious decision to complete something, I simply wouldn't, or maybe I couldn't.

When I was a year old, Mom made a poster with that quote. We still have it. The two feet by three feet poster is lime green in color, with a picture of me swimming in a blue pool. A six-month-old me with floaties on my arms and a grin on my face. You can say I was enjoying the swim. I was told that the picture was taken when I first tried swimming. Mom put the quote, "Whether you think you can or you can't, you're always right," for me to understand that we all eventually do what we decide to do.

Well, *almost*. The saying was accurate 90% of the time. But, sometimes, I would initially decide not to do something and still complete the task or vice versa. So, when I grew up, I added the word "almost," and the poster now said, "Whether you think you can or you think you can't, you are almost always right." So what started as a joke, stuck.

Navi, are you finished with homework?   Almost.
Are you ready for piano class?   Almost.
Is Nitya ready to go?   Almost.
Almost.

Today, one of my identities is that of a dancer, but it almost may not have been the case.

Mom and Dad had noticed me swaying to all sorts of songs even when I could barely walk. But my tendency to groove reached a different height that day. I was almost three. Wearing a long flowing *lehenga* adorned with white beads, I stared at the TV screen in our living room as the Bollywood playlist played on. It must have been Diwali; the house was lit with lots of *diyas* (earthen oil lamps). Mom was pregnant with Nitya. As the song, "Beedi Jalele" (a famous Hindi movie song) played on the TV screen, I got up and danced tiny but mighty moves. From what I've been told, my *thumkas* (a rhythmic dance step involving the waist) and sense of beat that day did not fall short, and we discovered my natural knack for dancing.

They put me into several dance classes. I always liked dancing but only in the free, party dancing type. Then I started *Bharatnatyam* (an Indian classical dance form) classes, which I also loved. Staying in *Aramandi* (the Indian version of a plié) for thirty minutes at a time was challenging. I would come home with aching pains but never complained about the class. I was four then.

Dad was in India a lot, establishing our real estate company, AtOnePlace. He was away, often, for three to four months. Mom was juggling work, household work, a seven-year-old me, and a three-year-old Nitya while I was juggling the different dance forms.

When I was eight, I met Mrs. Margherita Ryan – or Ms. Margie. She taught the "Western" dance styles in her academy Art in Motion. Though she taught many styles (ballet, jazz, lyrical, tap, and hip hop), she also taught basic Pilates, a mandatory class everyone had to take.

I tried Pilates for about two weeks and decided that it wasn't for me. It was a Wednesday, and Mom was ready to drive me to class. When she asked me if I was ready, I didn't respond. Not even "Almost." Instead, I threw a massive tantrum in the middle of our formal living room. On the black leather couches, I lay screaming. Finally, with my fists in tightly formed balls, I exploded. "This isn't for me. I can't do this. I don't like this...," I cried.

Still fussy, Mom picked me up and put me in her car. While driving, she sternly told me that I had to be respectful of Ms. Margie and attend the class no matter what. She wouldn't let me quit, though, she was fine with me just sitting on the side watching instead of actively participating.

That night, after I had cooled down a bit, we sat together on my bunk bed. On a blank sheet of paper, Mom had drawn a picture of the slide in our park. She explained, "There are many opportunities that we pursue that ultimately make us who we are." Then she cited examples from her own life. "I was a basketball player. I painted. I wish I had an opportunity to learn how to swim too. I like water but still don't feel comfortable in the pool. The things I wanted and pursued became my strengths, and those I didn't follow with full vigor were not. And sometimes we have to try a few times even to find out what we like. And it's worth the effort because knowing our strengths makes us feel good and confident to try even more new things. "

I turned to Mumma. "So, is dance my strength?" I asked.

"Perhaps. But you will never know if you don't try. See this..." She pointed to the 'climbing' section of the hand-drawn slide. "That's the learning years. You try different things and give them your best shot. You don't have to stick to it forever, but you have to try for a good enough time to give it your best shot once you start something."

"Just like in the park, we have to climb up the slide until we reach the top?" I asked.

She nodded.

"What's that then?" I pointed to the actual slide portion of the painting going down.

"That's the fun part. Once you put in the effort to reach the top, you enjoy the slide. You know winning and quitting are habits. Our minds and bodies get used to whichever feeling we offer them. So, make winning your habit. You will have to work towards it, but eventually, it will become a habit and not require as much effort."

I stuck with Ms. Margie's classes for years after. And I cherish both the ups and the downs of dancing till date.

Naveli's Diary

I think that night, I learned the concept of grit. And the virtue of not giving up when things seem difficult, instead attacking the difficult part head-on until it becomes easier. And before I realized, my vocabulary changed, and "almost" became "always." I also made a pact with Mom: from then on, anything we signed up for, we would stick to it for at least a year.

Manisha

The Slide

I have a vivid memory of a slide from my childhood years. I was in third grade and had joined a new school where I had made a new friend. Sometimes we would meet in the park in the evenings. She was always accompanied by her mother and her mischievous young brother. Her brother would jump around on the play structures and take the swings high up.

One day he attempted to climb the stairs of the tallest slide in the park. Usually, the older kids played on that structure. But unfortunately, he lost his balance and fell. Their mother ran to examine his bruised arm and knee and banished him from climbing the slide again.

Her family spoke Bengali. If ever he attempted to climb again, their mother would run towards him shouting, *"Podejabi,"* a Bengali term for "you will fall." He would obediently hold her hand and climb back down.

Their family had gone for a vacation then. I had often wondered if I could ever climb the slide. So that day, I decided to try. I had reached halfway through when the words "Podejabi" started ringing through my ears. I froze.

An older boy from the neighborhood was watching me from a distance. We were not friends, but we had occasionally talked in the park. He waved at me. Then, noticing that I was stationary, he stopped dribbling his ball and walked toward me until I heard his voice, "It is the same number of stairs going down as it is going up."

I remained quiet.

"You did great climbing so many steps. Now take a deep breath and try one more step."

I closed my eyes and took a deep breath. Then as I opened my eyes, I looked at him. He nodded, and I obediently abided. We repeated this exercise one step, and then to my pleasant surprise, I was at the top.

"Enjoy the slide; you have earned it." He waved at me and ran away, dribbling his ball again.

The thrill of achievement is intoxicating when we have worked hard for it. So, before my brain could reason me out, I was back in the line to go up again. The voice in my head was now playing "One more step" instead of "Podejabi." So, one step at a time, I reached the top and zipped down the slide I had thus earned.

The slide also earned me the regard of other kids in the park, and I became a frequent visitor on that slide. Then one day, I lost balance and fell. My friend's mother was quick to remind me of her advice. But I was addicted by now. No more scared of it; the fall made me curious to unearth the reason for falling. Then a few weeks later, I was back on the slide again, climbing first the stairs and later up the slide itself. This time, I experimented with gravity and felt the liquid inside my ear and its role in maintaining our balance.

Manisha's Diary

The slide taught how pushing through hard times often makes things easy. When I am in the middle of something, I focus only on giving it my best. Then, once it is over, I can always rethink and course-correct if needed.

I didn't have words to describe this notion to kids earlier until Wharton taught me about cognitive dissonance. We justify our doing and our not doing equally well to ourselves. Though the cognitive load that builds up in not doing is not worth the pain, the dissonance still takes over, and we keep justifying. Well, because we are smart and we can.

I recently paid the tax of wanting to finish a chapter yet postponing it, resulting in many restless nights. I am aware, yet still trapped in a human mind. Sometimes unable to climb up the slide.

Nitya

The Climb

My curious mind always pushed me to try new things, often at the cost of ditching the old ones. So, I phased through piano, Kathak dancing, soccer, swimming, ice skating, art, Bharatanatyam dancing, horseback riding, guitar, singing Indian and American style...You get the picture. Basically, any and everything familiar and obscure activity - I tried.

Initially, Mom encouraged me to explore. But one day, she imposed the "No Quitting" rule on me. It was simple; I could try whatever I wanted, but I had to stick to it for at least the school year. Mom explained that I was telling myself that I tried different things, but in actuality I wasn't giving each activity a fair chance. She said it is common to struggle, especially as we move beyond the basics. But eventually, we enjoy activities more as the climb becomes easier, and we get better at them. That is when the struggle converts into enjoyment.

Didi referred to this concept as "The Slide." I preferred calling it "The Climb" instead. So, with this conversation with Mom, I officially started my climb to the top of the slide. Well... multiple climbs.

It started in Pallavi Aunt's art classes. I had just told Mom I wanted to try art classes. And so, Mom researched a few programs and decided to pursue arts with Pallavi Aunty. I was too young to remember all the details now. A few years later, Pallavi Aunty told me how I had hidden behind Mom's legs, using them as windshield wipers for my protection. Aunty was initially apprehensive about taking me as her student, but when Mom insisted, Aunty gave in to Mom's conviction. I loved the art but not as much as interacting with Aunty or the other kids in the class.

I grew up watching Didi participate in all sorts of public speaking events. When I turned four, I felt ready and asked Mom to register me too. Before we knew it was time for my first speech. My first competition. Participants five and under. I was to talk about water. Mom had kept the setup as simple as possible. There was no memorization at all, just pictures. I had to go on stage and describe the images on paper. I practiced it a few times in front of the TV. I was ready. So, I walked up the stage confidently and turned to face the microphone. Then, as I investigated the deep sea of the audience in front, the water flowed down as tears instead. I waved to Mom to come close. As she joined me on stage, I hid behind her legs again. And when the administrators nudged me to try, I fled, running out of the room.

Since Didi was always confident in public, it took us time to understand that I feared public speaking. So, Mom enrolled me in Genius Kids with Rennu Aunty - a program that taught public speaking; and, indirectly, confidence. With that started another climb. We kept trying, and I finally delivered the speech, and it indeed felt like the top of the hill. I was excited; I gave the speech again at home to everyone who visited us. My confidence grew with every attempt. Twelve years later, I have climbed up from the shy girl hiding behind Mom's legs to a varsity debater, glad I didn't quit.

In hindsight, nothing is that black and white. While I continued art classes for ten years, won many competitions, and genuinely enjoyed the arts, I eventually dropped the course. The difference was, this time, I wasn't quitting out of fear. This time, I chose and prioritized exploring the other interests I wanted to pursue for now. With the confidence that as my calendar frees up, I can reimmerse in arts again.

For years, a hand-sketched diagram of a climb/ or a slide had been a permanent fixture on our corkboard. That paper has now gone, leaving just the image engraved in my mind forever.

In middle school, I developed a liking for theater and dance. I had learned to strive to give everything my very best by now. So fresh into seventh grade, I decided to try straight for the lead role in my first semester of drama. There was no harm in trying, but I had shallow hopes of getting it. On the other hand, Mom seemed confident that I could earn it if I put in my all. Which I did.

The night before the audition, I went to her to show her my monologue. As I recited it confidently, Mom looked perplexed. I was generally animated with facial expressions in day-to-day life. Mom could sense that I was holding back. She told me to exaggerate my movements, "like this," she showed, modeling odd movements. "No, it's okay," I said, believing that I would look like a fool in front of all my peers if I did that. That's when she asked me to sit, and so I did. She then asked how much I wanted that lead role. And when I confirmed I really did want it, she explained that acting is about owning the character. If the character was loud, I had to display noticeable expressions to do justice, even if it felt odd. I stood no chance unless I gave it my best. And I deserved a reasonable chance of getting the role if I tried with full conviction without holding anything back.

The next day I went in and delivered the monologue. I was somewhat worried, so I dumbed down the version Mom had suggested. But still, mine was the most exaggerated of my peers. I received many compliments for my accentuation, and when the cast list came out, my name filled the row for the lead role.

Another of my climbs was towards dancing. While Didi was pursuing multiple different dance styles, I decided to stick to Bollywood dance to keep space for my other interests. Our dance teacher taught us to focus on two main things: expression and movement. And while I seemed to excel in facial expressions, just as I had in acting, my physical movements were not as clean. Didi was naturally gifted at both, though she used to lean more towards finessing her techniques and sometimes ignored her expressions.

Unfortunately, in this climb up, what started as admiration for Didi, slowly turned into envy. A combination of backhanded comments at parties like "Naveli is an outstanding dancer and Nitya... your expressions were superb," and perhaps, a sprout of sibling rivalry that emerges in growing years. Somehow, people in our community developed a habit of comparing us, and somehow, I did too.

In the summer before seventh grade, I joined a new dance troupe, Gurus of Dance. Didi was already part of the troupe and had played the lead dancer and actress for one of their professional productions. She was well-established. Mom saw an opportunity for me to participate in an upcoming nationwide dance competition and for the two of us to bond back again through that experience. I practiced hard, dancing even on blistered feet, and finally cleared the audition.

I was then the only new member of an elite dance team. Unfortunately, the same pattern of comparison followed there as well. Some commented that I didn't deserve to be part of the troupe. What hurt me the most was when someone noted that they heard Didi also agree that I was yet to earn my spot. When confronted, Didi denied the allegation, and I wasn't sure whom to believe.

At home, Mom also seemed to compare me to Didi, at least those days. As per her, she was encouraging us to learn from each other. Unfortunately, it fostered nothing but negativity on my end. My constant desire to "earn my spot" made me work hard without ever appreciating the progress I was already making. While this climb improved my skill, it bogged my self-esteem, and my sarcasm brought down Didi's esteem.

One day my new teacher, Aditya, pulled me aside for a talk. While Mom taught me to strive to be my best, Aditya taught me the nuance of trying too hard. He reminded me that I was an individual, not just Didi's sister. He told me I had the determination and willpower to excel. But in constantly comparing myself to Didi, I had forgotten that we both could strive together.

I knew that I needed to improve on many fronts, but I stopped feeling like I wasn't good enough. I decided to move to the front during our practice sessions, where I could see Aditya clearly. Instead of watching Didi, I now observed Aditya's movements. I also started noticing Didi's efforts and her natural grace in movements. She welcomed me with open arms at every step into her established friend groups, easing my struggles as the new person and helping me blend in with the team.

My learning accelerated. Didi was officially also the teacher's assistant for some dances. She gave me private sessions at home where she taught me to stretch more, increase flexibility, and improve my movement. This isn't to say it was all easy, as I'd still feel belittled by Didi in her coaching sessions when she offered constructive criticism. We started discussing our feelings candidly. I learned that comparison was neither required nor constructive. I, in fact, had the advantage of having a teacher at my disposal anytime. She also realized that I had grown up and learned to treat me as such.

After weeks of arduous preparatory practice sessions, Aditya drafted a small group for a crucial piece of the presentation. Again, of course, Didi was chosen... but this time, so was I. Gossip still spread, questioning my merit. I didn't care as Aditya assured me that I had earned my spot.

Nitya's Diary

It's funny how animated childhood movies can be unexpectedly the most insightful. This lesson I took years to learn was encompassed by Buster Moon's one quote; "You know what's great about hitting rock bottom, there's only one way left to go, and that's up!"

The climb with Aditya gave me a fresh perspective - we must work to reach the top while also appreciating our progress. Most importantly, it taught me that while it's essential to learn from others, the only person I need to compare myself with is the person I aspire to become.

I've learned a lot through climbing these slides, figuratively and literally. To try before quitting. To silence my fear of failing with my actions. To strive to be my best self rather than comparing myself with others.

The amusing part also is that the task always seems much more daunting until I start it. And as I master it seems to automatically diminish in its capacity to overwhelm me.

Buster Moon said it best; "You know what's great about hitting rock bottom, there's only one way left to go, and that's up!"

Harry Potter

Overcome fears. Give life a full shot at living.

Manisha

The pandemic had created a new level of chaos and uncertainty. I spent more than fourteen hours a day preparing for the launch. Every discussion needed to be planned and scheduled ahead, as walking into somebody's room to vet an idea was no more an option.

It felt good to relive old moments with my girls amidst the hustle and bustle of uncertainties. I wished for them to strengthen their conviction to overcome fears through this experience. Life deserves a full shot at living. But unfortunately, the dichotomy of current-day living lets life come in its own way. The worry about our future or our kid's future grooms millions of us to choose an artificial sense of comfort. Like a machine, we keep trading time for money, and happiness for stability, and bit by bit, death in the form of fear, anxiety, and worry rules our lives. As we live this death-led life, we let our kids watch, for them to inherit this lifestyle from us.

Stress is a powerful teacher. As such, I never dealt with poverty, life-threatening wars, orphanages, or incarcerations. But still, life went through its ups and downs, and in its wake, it taught me to face fears head-on.

While growing up, Papa's (my father) frequent transfers made change the only constant. On the first day at a new school, Mummy would remind us, "You can make new friends by helping them first." With that mantra, Ankur (my brother) and I ventured into unknown territories to live Papa's teaching - convert every "can you?" to "why can't I." By the time I completed twelfth, cycling through eight schools, fear of the unknown had evolved into an excitement to explore.

The explorations did come at a cost. For example, Papa's decision to move at the end of ninth grade made me forgo the opportunity to become the "head girl," the ultimate prestige symbol for the senior-most students then. Indian schools were structured differently, with tenth being the senior-most year in secondary schools. The hurt was deep. But I had to move on and focus on landing in a good school in the new city.

We moved. Admissions in the tenth grade were complex. The school's prestige depended on the results of the nationwide board exam conducted in the tenth grade. Papa's convincing skills, paired with my academic ability, and some luck helped us gain admission to Nirmala Convent School, beautifully located in a modest town called Haldwani at the foothills of Nainital.

I became that new girl in class ten; neither the school nor the town had seen such a child before. People were amicable, though I desperately missed the comfort of my old school and friends. Mummy and Papa repeatedly encouraged us to adapt. I found solace in my studies. News traveled fast in small towns as I topped the quarterly exams. Watchful eyes became friendlier; I gained respect from my teachers and made friends quickly, several of whom I am still in touch with. I was told later that some teachers had recommended my name for that year's yet forming student council. The hurt was less painful this time as I read the board's decision, "her candidacy has merit, but she is too new to be considered per the school policy." Like everything, practice made even resilience stronger.

The flourishing friendships dwarfed the pain of losing the "Head Girl" title, that I had deeply desired and lost twice. New doors kept opening, and I kept jumping "all in." Like a Swiss knife, I wanted to develop many capabilities even if I was known only for one.

We lived in another city, Rudrapur, and had to pass through a scenic jungle over an hour-long ride to our school in Haldwani. My friend's mom had checked the board results on our behalf and announced loudly that I was her daughter in her jubilation. Confusion grew as I, oblivious to this, introduced my real mom to my friends later as we reached school. No matter how much time flies, the memory of the warm group hug and the loud celebratory exchanges from people, strangers just a year back, remains vivid like fresh paint.

We had heard the saying, "It takes a village to raise a child." That year, we experienced the village Haldwani had created with its open lush green arms as we went through all the trying and tiring turbulence. A little girl from a traditional joint family left Haldwani with an expanded imagination and a circle of lifelong friends.

Nitya

I used to love dogs. I begged to have one of my own. There was something about combing out their soft, luscious hair between my fingers. They say that dogs are a man's best friend, and at that age, I used to agree until one night when everything changed.

I was seven years old then. Over my summer break, I joined my dad on his India trip. We visited my cousins in Delhi, with whom I built fond memories. We drove to their home at night when the sun was settling down. As I attempted to sleep, I could experience the sounds and smells of India. First, the loud honking as people competed on their abilities to honk the most. Next, the aromas of the watered-down dirt drying mixed with the smell of the hot, humid, muggy air made it impossible to sleep. Then there were the endless tapping noises at our window (from people selling flowers and gadgets). The best part was that all this happened at a convenient time when the road was jammed entirely, making our escape slow and painful. We finally reached.

We were immediately greeted by guards, maids, and cooks. Next, we met Thouji (my dad's older cousin), Taiji (his wife), Kanha Bhaiya (their son), and Honey Di (their daughter). We sat at a long dining table for a nice steamy meal, after which we went upstairs to sleep.

Their house was gated, more gorgeous, and expansive than any other I'd ever lived in. A theater room with reclinable seats, a game room, a pool, and a lush garden were in the backyard. But the biggest reason I liked being there was their big, fluffy, black dog. So while my dad had plans to visit other places, I insisted on staying back the following day.

I was alone with Kanha Bhaiya, about seven years older than me.

Confident in my passion for dogs, we went to give a treat to the gorgeous dog. He gave the dog a treat, then gave me one, indicating me to feed it, and left the room to get more. As I peered forward excitedly, the dog advanced closer towards the treat in my left hand. Perhaps nervous, he swerved and bit the topmost forearm under my elbow, leaving tooth marks and blood dripping.

I initially shrieked, paralyzed with shock, then fearfully ran down the endless stairs. Bhaiya called the maids for water and our parents. It took them thirty minutes to come back by when the bleeding had stopped. I was rushed to the hospital. A shot and six stitches later, I had developed two new fears: dogs and needles. Scars of teeth marks, the size of a dime, reminded me of that day and the fear it bred.

Unfortunately for me, while I feared dogs, I loved art classes. And my teacher at the time, Pallavi Aunty, had a tiny white Maltese, Frosty. Not wanting to let the fear overtake my passions, Mom and I decided to deal with it head-on. The first time took a while. But with the help of Pallavi Aunt's endless empathy, I finally pet Frosty. We made it a ritual - for me to pet Frosty at the beginning and end of every class. Soon Frosty and I became good friends. Pallavi Aunty not only helped me immerse in the arts but also helped me overcome my fear. More than a teacher, she is a friend and a pillar who changed my life.

Gradually, I became more comfortable with small dogs and later the big ones. When I travel to India, where street animals roam freely, I now find cuteness in all animals ranging from monkeys and dogs to cows and birds.

Then came the pandemic, where newfound boredom drove families to desire a pet. Dad was still uncomfortable with the idea of keeping a pet dog. Finally, as friends and family around adopted dogs, my family agreed to let me sit them. After a few days of dog-sitting, my thirst was somewhat quenched. But then came Casper to stay with us for a month while the family visited India. A tiny old rescue dog, Casper was always on guard. Challenging to get along with initially, he eventually adopted us as we became his fan. When he left our home, we felt lonelier. We met him again, but it wasn't enough. My ambitions for getting a dog were renewed.

On a whim, I decided to convince everyone. So, I cooked dinner, ensuring we all ate together that night, and then pulled out a six-page packet that I had made earlier that morning. It had reasons to get a dog (for health and family), preemptive rebuttals to objections I had predicted (like dealing with allergies to dog hair, cost, how will we take care, etc.), and suggestions for us as a family to sustain the new lifestyle.

While the process wasn't as direct as I had hoped, everyone agreed eventually.

Our research compelled us to adopt or rescue, and not custom breed. After much unfruitful search through rescue homes, we met Zoey and Zion when Sherry Aunty connected us with their earlier owners. Unable to care for them, they scheduled the rescue home to take Zoey and Zion away. The Zs immediately adopted us, and within hours they were in our house, not yet prepared for dogs then. Eventually, everything fell in place. Zs became the center of our conversations. Dad overcame his fears and now ritually says good morning and good night to them and frequent belly rubs and massages.

Naveli

A confident dancer, I aimed to be a triple threat. When we learned about Kronos' auditions, a professional musical production, I was still working on my acting skills. Mom came to pick me up after class, and Aachu, my friend-turned-brother, mentioned that they were driving down straight to auditions. He was interested in the male lead and encouraged me to try for the female lead. I was keen yet full of self-doubt.

Mom and I were in our car alone. My immediate response? "I won't get it."

"Are you 100% sure of that?" Mom asked.

"I am not ready to audition. I don't even know this troupe. Wouldn't they choose one of their own?"

"Well, you won't know if you don't try. Good troupes tend to choose the deserving, their own, or newcomers capable of becoming their own."

"But I don't have a scene I have memorized."

"I will drive you down. You look up some scenes on your phone and practice in the car with me. Also, audition for both acting and dance; it's a musical."

Both of us sat silent for a couple of minutes, reflecting. Finally, I nodded, reached out for my phone, and punched the new address in the GPS.

I landed the lead dancer and actress role in Kronos and got an opportunity to train under Aditya Patel. Under his guidance, I finessed my steps and speech to prove my worth, earn their respect, and become one of their own. Tenth grade was a grueling year with ten to twenty hours of practice after school each week for almost eight months. I conquered my fears through hard work and the guidance of my friends, teachers, and family. It's not that I don't fear anything now. But I have figured out a system to not let my fears come in my way.

I continued with Aditya, graduated from the academy, and today I teach with him.

Naveli's Diary

Modern-day society has evolved to favor stability, which instills a fear of the unknown from a young age. I am lucky to have parents who offered a lifestyle where exploring became a game, winning an addiction, and learning from failures' strength. I hope to help my friends overcome their fears as well and give life a full shot at living.

In the Kitchen

The day was windy. We decided to skip the trampoline and stay indoors. The girls were craving pasta, which led all three of us towards the kitchen.

"Naveli, fetch the pasta, Nitya, get the veggies," I suggested as I prepared to unload the dishwasher.

As Naveli returned from the pantry, I was bent on my knees, searching for the pasta boiler behind the pressure cooker.

"Mom, I used to fear the pressure cooker, right?" Naveli asked.

"Indeed, every time the whistle blew, you would come running and wrap yourself around my legs. Interestingly, we used to play the game of hugs those days, So, it took me a while to understand that these hugs were fear-inspired," I confirmed.

"How did I overcome that fear?" she asked.

"We embarked on a journey to overcome the 'whistle fear.' I would hold you and stand at a safe distance from the cooker, waiting for the whistle to blow."

"I will chop veggies," Navi suggested and directed Nitya to scrape sun-dried tomatoes out of the bottle.

I continued as nostalgia kicked in." You would open just one eye as the whistle started dancing. So we cooked up stories of the pulses boiling inside and with each whistle becoming softer for our teeth. Since you like dancing, we also compared the whistle to a ballet dancer twirling and spinning. And then we started alluding to the whistle sounds as the applause. We were crazy - vapors became painters once as the cooker splashed the yellow turmeric water and lentils all around the stove."

They started dancing, making gestures with the knife and the spatula. "You must have played this game diligently until I got over my fear," Naveli smiled.

I nodded. "Yup. Later when the whistle blew, you would command me to hit it with a wooden spatula like a ship's captain to release its steam. Thanks to our 'whistle game,' we often had overcooked lentils for dinner."

"I remember Nitya used to fear the cooker. She burst out in loud tears once when she wasn't even a year old. She couldn't speak then, right?" Naveli asked.

I nodded in agreement.

"I remember making crazy facial expressions as the whistle blew until she stopped crying and started laughing."

"Indeed. You were a good sister. You conditioned her to ignore the cooker. In fact, it became a toy for her, and a few days later, we heard Nitya burst out again, this time with excitement-filled laughter as the pressure cooker whistle blew." I kissed Naveli.

Nitya had been quietly loading the dishwasher. "How did you help us overcome the Harry Potter fear, Mom?" she asked.

"You were quite young then." I looked at Nitya.

"Yes, I had just started kindergarten." She saved me from trying to remember.

"Yup. Didi was in fourth grade. The series had become the talk of the town and somehow become a fear factor for us," Naveli chimed in.

"A new art studio had opened in our vicinity. The artist-teacher seemed different. So, I took both of you to try one Friday evening. Instead of handholding and directing you to recreate preselected pieces, she gave you a blank sheet. Then, she pointed you to the color table full of crayons, a few pastels, and watercolors and asked you to create something.

"'ANYTHING?' Nitya had asked. Her eyes were wide, matching her smile running from ear to ear.

"'ANYTHING,' the art teacher had responded with the same big smile.

"You picked the green pastel and made a few hills covering the top–third of the page. Then used the gray crayon to make rough strokes on the left side of the paper. Then you picked the gray pastel and rubbed it hard on the same patch, from the left to almost the center of the sheet. The powdered pastel had started coming off like a cloud of smoke when you finally dropped it. And then meticulously sketched a horse-like figure in front of the muddy gray patch," I narrated to her as I moved closer to pick a knife from the dishwasher.

Moving back towards the stove where Naveli was chopping the veggies, I continued, "Naveli sat on a different side of the room. She sketched a square figure with many eyes and legs. All of them held each other in a tight embrace.

"When the teacher asked you to name your artworks, Nitya quickly announced, 'The horse is running, and the dust is coming,' while Naveli called her piece 'Monsters can hug.'

"I was so proud of you two. I still am."

"We celebrated with ice cream and discussed the joys of creative explorations. We brainstormed wilder monsters who could hug and the mess of dust they could create. One string of thought led to another."

I was midway through when Naveli finished my sentence, "And you opportunistically steered it towards J.K. Rowling's creations."

"Guilty as charged. We discussed how Harry Potter and all the witches were also imaginary creations. Somehow, you both agreed to watch a Harry Potter movie to get more painting ideas."

"We watched on the sofa with you in the center, and we discussed what might have gone through J.K. Rowling's head when sketching out the scary scenes."

"Yes, and one movie at a time, we completed the entire series," Naveli added, "I then read all the volumes, including the last one that was not yet picturized. But you were too young to read."

Naveli and I thought that to be a good conclusion of the story as we settled at the round table to relish the freshly cooked pasta.

Then Nitya told us something new. "You don't know this. Didi got over her fear of Harry Potter, but I developed a deep fear of bathrooms and reflections in mirrors at night through this experience. And I feared entering the school toilets for many days."

It had been years since. All we could feel and say now was, "Sorry."

Manisha's Diary

Coaching is contagious. Our conversations, designed to help them navigate fears, have taken a 180-degree turn. They now keep me accountable for overcoming my fears. My explorer gene might have been the most active initially though we have now become a family of explorers. "Darte darete kar lenge" (we will do it even if we fear it) has become a family value. From adventure sports to new classes, experiences, and entrepreneurship, we have learned to try.

On a recent trip to the Dominican Republic, we all ventured into snorkeling. Naveli and Nitya encouraged Gunjan and me to try the deep waters. But unfortunately, I still can't swim. So, I was hesitant to let go of my second hand off the boat until I heard the two of them repeating my message back to me, "Mom, you know what you have to do, face your fears head-on. You can't let it rule you."

I had to let go. Although I snorkeled, holding a local diver's hand, I felt more alive than I had in a long time. The thrill of letting go and finally being able to do something I had been dreaming of for years. A heavy weight now lifted off my chest and inspired me to learn swimming. Someday that day too shall come.

Sometimes despite trying, we fail. Had I only known what Nitya went through earlier, I could have tried better or taken a different approach with her. Parenting two kids is doing two different jobs, not the same job done twice. Sometimes I remember that, and sometimes I still forget.

Nitya's Diary

I was scared then. And hurt later that nobody understood my fear of the bathroom mirrors. Maybe I could have shared clearly like I did today. But thanks to Harry Potter, we did learn to tame our fears and banish them with an invisibility cloak. I never want to be held *back from pursuing my passions and dreams again due to a silly overcomable fear.*

The Harry Potter books, read, and reread, torn in the covers, now sit in our library's memorabilia section.

Coexistence

Families are complex units, as are humans.

When intentional, we can create mutually beneficial experiences. When ignorant, the interplay of our emotions, exposures, and aspirations can create unintentional consequences. The choice is entirely ours.

Over the last several months, our emails flooded with updates and training on diversity and equity. Across the board, workplaces, universities, and schools were encouraged to be inclusive in our actions. As a result, some of our conversations gravitated towards these topics.

As we narrated our stories, we discovered how seemingly inconsequential actions of a family member had lasting consequences on another, even in an ordinary family like ours. These early experiences at home had played a critical role in shaping us and our biases. Candid conversations provided the context to see things in the right light.

Metals

Make music or make noise.

Naveli

Metals

As much as a family is supposed to be a unit reflective of the same ideals and aspirations, it poses its own challenges too. It's convenient to group together a unit, even though every individual has their own personality and truths. As we progress on our personal journeys, understanding others often becomes a challenge, as clashing egos get in the way. I, too, am guilty of distrusting my family.

It was July 2021. An incoming junior in college. Taking summer courses. I had overloaded myself with three challenging classes on top of a summer internship. I was also helping at the home front and trying to spend more time with family. I was constantly busy, just like every other family member. Nitya had SAT prep. Dad was constantly at work, trying to launch his new company, HeartyyFresh. Mom was busy with her job at Oracle and her passion project, Sakra.

In addition, we had my brother Ainesh's wedding. At a dance class, I met him and Aachu, his younger brother. Even though we are not related by blood, we are close like siblings are. Ainesh Bhaiya and Orma Bhabhi (his bride) married twice. We all enjoyed the California wedding performed as per the North Indian rituals.

By July 28th, Mom and I were in Pittsburgh, Pennsylvania, for Ainesh Bhaiya's second wedding ceremony, this time following the South Indian traditions of Orma's family. Unfortunately, those were also the dates for the final exams for my courses. I was keen to fully participate in all the events leading up to the wedding. That week might have been one of the most stressful yet fun weeks of my life.

Fully knowing that I had to be prepared ahead, I studied the concepts in advance. And revised them during the flight. On July 29th morning, I took the CHE 2C final exam in my hotel room before the Sangeet. Then another final on July 30th while all decked up in my white and gold Kasavu saree with hand-stitched green embroidery. My last final was a group paper. I proactively told my group about the wedding on the first day of the group assignment. We divided the paper into individual sections, with me taking the lead on the submission draft. I had completed my part before flying to Pittsburg. So, I was done. But Mom was anxious about why I wasn't worried about that last final. So, she questioned why I wasn't actively working on it? Why was I at the reception dancing instead?

We had planned an extra day post the ceremonies to explore Pittsburg together. So for all of Saturday, even though we wanted to enjoy our time in Pittsburg and sightsee, we had constant small arguments. Most around this exact topic. None of us budged.

At 3:00 a.m., in the fifteen-minute Uber ride back from Ainesh and Orma's apartment near downtown Pittsburgh to our hotel room, I poured my emotion into this poem on the Notes app on my iPhone.

Metals
It feels like I hurt you. But to please you.
I thought I learned from my mistakes
And turned around my life just trying
Though nothing seemed to phase you. Or touch you.
I thought I made strives,
Yet somehow, only you couldn't see. It's true.
Silver and gold don't mix well
No color formed, yet symmetry still
A paradise made. No words found. Effective.
Just unknown.
I thought metals look alike. Feel alike.
Uniqueness flows with hints of similarity.
You please me. I please you.
You hurt me. I hurt you.
Always alike but still not the same.

Metals.

That's what Mom and I were. Clashing. Yet it felt like we were cut from the same cloth. Together yet separate. I felt alienated and misunderstood by her and my family. I wondered; didn't I do everything right?

By 5:00 a.m., we had to check out and head to the airport; our flight was in two hours, and we were silent, not speaking to each other.

Though I did my best to be on top of my work and prioritize, I always felt like I was doing something wrong. It wasn't up to Mom's standards or maybe her hopes for me. The argument was over. She didn't understand my way of handling things, and I couldn't comprehend hers. But it wasn't the first time we had carried on this kind of explosive conversation.

Conversations are only valuable when we truly listen and speak to each other openly and honestly. I have learned that the only way to correctly resolve such issues is to talk it out.

By 9:00 a.m., Mom and I were as well-rested as we could be on a cramped seat on an airplane flight. More than anything, we were ready to talk without getting inflicted with emotions and fatigue. I started, "It's not a justification, but I genuinely thought this was the best way to handle finals. I finished everything I was responsible for. I delegated. I tried Mumma. And I think it went well. We received an A on the paper. So, if I did all of that, what did I do wrong? I don't get it. I thought I learned and am still learning. But if these are my efforts, are they wrong?"

She took a second, looked at me through her red-framed glasses, and held my hand. "Navi, I'm not saying you shouldn't delegate. I'm not saying that you handled finals wrongly. I am very proud of the way you focused and prioritized finals during such a hectic weekend. I just don't know why you reacted that way when I asked you about your last final."

I was confused. Did I react badly? What was so off-putting that caused this entire fight? "What do you mean?"

Mumma responded, "You said you had it all under control and for me to not worry. You told me that I should trust you, and you were confident that you would get a good grade because you had done your part well, and now it was up to the group."

I looked at her, slowly realizing what I thought I had done wrong. She said, "You can't promise or expect a good grade that way. You can't rely solely on having finished 'your part' of the paper, primarily since you are graded as a group. You were okay leaving your grade – your future– in the hands of others. All I wanted was for you to want to go back and check in with your teammates. Make sure the submission is okay from your perspective. But you justified and didn't listen. You were closed off. How could I trust that you were not repeating your old mistakes again?"

I now understood. I had a history of wanting to do well academically but, at times, not being the most driven or disciplined about it. The confusion and uncertainty are all she wanted to alleviate for both of us. Angst and stress could have been minimized had we been open and honest with each other all along. That's all that was needed. And yet, it took us three and a half days to resolve a simple conflict.

After we talked it out during the flight, I showed Mumma *Metals*. She chuckled, "Indeed. We are metals, you and me. … But you are gold. You better be."

Nitya

Three and a Half

Didi always told me I was lucky to be younger. Less stress, I guess… less responsibility and expectation. She walked me to art classes, helped me heat up food when our parents were working, and introduced me to the trendy YouTubers. I was grateful, of course.

At the same time, I also noticed her pride when saying she was four years older than me whenever the question was posed. "Three and a half," I would correct. "Same thing," she would respond. So, in my mind, it was pretty much set: Didi had the choice to take care of me, which she opted for, and as a result, gained the power to act like my second mom, which she exercised with pride. Though I enjoyed learning new things from her, the criticism and judgment alongside irritated me at times.

It felt like I lived an off-brand revision of Didi's life, a slightly different touch to the same old story, a reprised version of an old song.

I was lucky to get some freedom earlier than her. Some because Mom and Dad grew into their not-so-new role of being parents. Others because Didi had already fought the battles for us three and a half years before I could. For example, when shall we get our phones, how much screen time was allowed, how late we could stay out, etc.?

Mom had always encouraged an open conversation forum if we maintained an amicable decorum. Didi and I abided. Well.. not always. Like other siblings, we relayed our opinions and thoughts to each other. But the second half of Mom's rule was up for debate. We fought loud, vocally, and occasionally would get carried away and get a little physical. Physical fights in our house meant a minor hit or a wrist grab, which I would opportunistically milk with tears for sympathy from the parental audience. That is one bonus of being younger - a chance to play innocent.

While some may view fighting as messy and punishment-worthy, Mom always took the approach of reflection over detention. She helped us address our negativity differently through poised communication. Her deadliest punishments often were for us to sit in a corner and write down our actions and reflections on how we made the other person feel. Then we had to share our perspectives calmly, no matter how angry we felt inside. Over time we started understanding each other and became comfortable with discussing uncomfortable topics even without Mom around.

While Dad was in India, Mom split her time between her work and us. She often said that family is a bond you can never break and that the three of us were each other's best friends. I would nod in agreement, but I never truly understood what she meant. Instead, I saw the family as family and friends as friends. My young, naive brain was plain, black, white, and straightforward. Often my friends commented on how lucky I was to be so close with Didi. Finally, I started realizing the blessing of being a part of a family that normalized the awkward conversations as much as the fun ones.

I would like to think that by the time I was in middle school and Didi in high school, we had begun to understand the benefits and hardships of both sides of our equation, the old and the young. Slowly but surely, my perspective had changed. Rather than feeling sad about inheriting second-hand clothes, I was excited to get stylish clothes before my friends did. My new outlook (for the most part) now was that Didi walked so that I could run. I was becoming increasingly grateful for her.

Then our fights increased again. Officially we both share a room. But over the years, especially as Didi entered high school, we initially started studying in different rooms and then sleeping there. Before anyone knew it, we started living separately in two separate rooms. And then slowly, we also started closing our doors. As our fights increased, Mom forced us to settle back in our room and nagged us to talk to each other constantly. We took it lightly until she gave us an ultimatum. Start earning and paying the rent if you want to use other rooms. Of course, she was joking, but her message drove home at supersonic speed.

Mom's methods worked. From staying silent around each other, we advanced to fighting, conversing, understanding, and finally became a cohesive team yet again. The more I learned about Didi, the more I became incredibly proud to be The Naveli Garg's sister. So much so that I spoke of her positive attributes in awe to my friends. I made sisterly gifts for her like a tile that said "sister by chance, friends by choice" inspired by Liv and Maddie that to this date lives on our fridge. And in January of 2020, I wrote this song.

Your life was all bright.
Then I took the spotlight.
You were older
Bolder
I wanted your life.
But then I realized it all came at a price.
Having to
Shut up,
Sit up,

Give up my life.
Indeed, it came at a price.
More chores to divide,
Making meals twice,
Feeding me rice,
Still, you continued to love me most of the time.
To suffice,
Sacrifice,
The things that you like.
For a sister
Not a mister,
Who annoyed you,
Destroyed your social life.
Still, you continued to love me most of the time.
Taking care of me,
Ever since you were three.
Ever since you've been free.
Even when I was mean.
I would chill with your friends
Tell them your stories.
Making,
Your nightmares a reality,
And your life a prophecy.
And instead of leaving me through all this process,
To date, you still take me to classes.

Most recently though, I got Didi a Christmas present in 2021. When I was younger, I used to wear a necklace with a charm depicting the Indian God, Ganesh. Whenever I needed help or felt lonely, I knew I could simply talk to Ganesh. So as college was getting stressful for Didi and she began feeling homesick, I decided to get her a necklace similar to that of my childhood self. Except this necklace had a picture of our family including Zoey and Zion, our dogs, so that she would know we were always by her side rooting for her.

I would never have been able to understand my sister the way I do now if I hadn't spent the time and effort to profoundly get to know the wonderful person she is.

Nitya's Diary

It is indeed difficult to hate someone when you know their stories. Sometimes you love them even more as I now feel for Didi. This is not to say there weren't and aren't bumps in our road, but for the most part, I am pretty clear that being four years younger isn't the worst thing in the world.

Manisha

Vikram and Beetal

This memory goes back to the year we lived with our joint family in Sirsa, Haryana in India. I was back from school. It was late afternoon, about 4:00 p.m. Our joint family had finished lunch, and I neatly placed the washed dishes back on the kitchen racks, as was my daily chore. My Mom and aunts had stepped out to the local market to run errands. My brother and cousin were playing on the rooftop.

My grandma was napping in her usual spot; her bed pulled out on the veranda to enjoy the afternoon sun, when the doorbell rang. I remember opening the door to greet an elderly neighborhood aunt who followed me to meet Grandma. After exchanging greetings, they settled in for chitchat.

I remember the aunt praising in Hindi, "girls are such a blessing. She is doing housework when the boys are playing." Amma (my grandma) had ignored the comment.

After a brief pause, the aunt commented again, "She is pretty. Takes after you."

This time Grandma snapped back, "*Koi naa. Main to ghandi soni thi.*" (Not at all. I was very beautiful in my youth.)

My grandma had continued to refute the aunt's comment. "*Ladke kama ke layenge. Naam kamayenge. Yeh to chali jayegi.*" (The boys will earn. They will bring fame. She will marry off.)

As I continued to stack the dishes, I remember thinking that I may not be pretty, but I will come first in my class. I was seven years old, in second grade then.

Amidst many hazy memories, I sometimes relive vivid glimpses of my past. Even though we lived in Sirsa for a year, I have fond memories of the brick red school building surrounded by the vast playground with semi-green-semi-dried grass beds. Lunchtimes at school were fun with a gang of friends atop the swings and play structures. My friends looked upon me for guidance. My ability to help them made me feel good. Not all subjects came easy to me, but I could sit through hours and study until I got them.

Home was different. I went into an automatic gear shift on the bus from school back home. Home was the place to fly under the radar and avoid giving Amma any chance to notice anything that would start another distasteful debate. Amma, by the way, was terrific for several of the other family members, especially her youngest son and my male cousins. My existence as a girl child had created a unique position in her court, for not just me but also my parents.

At home, my escape post-homework used to be at our neighbor's house. The houses in India are often joined, making it easy to hop from one roof to another. Our neighbors were inferior to us on the socio-economic graph. They looked upon us, including me, with the utmost respect. They had a two-year-old daughter, Pooja - petite, sweet, naïve. I loved playing with her. She loved hearing stories, so I would often narrate stories from my small collection of books.

One day, I read a story from the Vikram and Beetal series where Vikram was a king and Beetal a ghost hanging from a tree. These stories had moral science lessons. Kids were encouraged to read them. I used to animate the characters for Pooja in my storytelling. So I walked in a kingly manner for Vikram's dialogues and growled as Beetal might as he escaped yet again from Vikram's grip. Pooja would come running to me after Beetal's devious laughter.

The next day Pooja was quiet. Her mom whispered that Pooja had nightmares. I briefly wondered if there was a connection between the story and the nightmares and ignored the thought. Fortunately, her mom was never around for our story sessions to make the link, and Pooja was too young to comprehend the connection.

A few weeks passed. Another incident happened at home. Amma picked up another fight with my mom commanding her to serve me tea and the boys the expensive milk. Mom had respectfully retaliated by splitting the share of milk offered to my brother between the two of us. At the same time, my aunts served my male cousins a full glass of milk each as I observed silently.

Next Sunday, when Pooja asked for a story, I narrated another story from the Vikram Beetal series, this time more animated than ever.

I did not see Pooja during the week as my exams were on. Later, when I visited her the following weekend, I learned about her week-long fever. She was quiet. And although she still liked cuddling with me, she was not interested in stories anymore. Finally, Pooja fell asleep holding my hand. As I was about to leave, her mother made a polite request in fearful whispers, "I am thankful that you play with Pooja, but could you please not tell any scary stories to her. She wakes up, scared of Beetal." I was dumbstruck. Scared. Ashamed to say aloud what I had understood through those whispers. To escape the Beetal in my life, I had become one in Pooja's life.

Guilt-filled shame kept me restless and sleepless for many moons. This was my time to go silent.

Silence has many merits. As I silenced the cacophony of noises coming from my vocal cords, I also silenced the noises around me, enabling me to observe and understand the serpentine-like social constructs that inundate our daily lives. I started noticing the stark difference in expectations of men and women. Even amongst all my dad's brothers, I witnessed the special treatment the youngest one enjoyed. There were also tiers of hierarchy in kids. My younger male cousin had a higher status over my brother as their mom brought dowry for the family. In contrast, my mom came with double master's degrees, a brain she insisted on using, and the courage to question. I also observed the irony in the adults ridiculing kids for not studying when they were the ones to belittle my mom's education.

There was also a hierarchy outside of our family. Our societal status was higher than our back-door neighbors and superior to our maids and servants. Birth itself was a lottery. No one was offered the choice to sit out - cards were dealt, rules announced, and everyone was ordered to play. My cards scored me low on the gender rule and high on the socio-economic rules. Somehow Amma, perhaps with her commanding personality, had claimed the throne, and everyone in the family had surrendered to her.

The more I observed, the more my curiosity grew. Finally, borne under the burden of my own questions, I prepared to confront Amma. I may have lost the birth lottery, but still I didn't want to yield to Amma's power of bringing out the devious Beetal in me.

Courage came later, compassion sooner as I questioned Amma for Pooja's sake. Though she didn't recede, Papa and Mummy decided to move out of the joint family home. Pooja got freedom from her Beetal, and I gained the confidence to fight back when things felt wrong.

Manisha's Diary

Human psychology plays mischievous games. We are unbound by nature yet bound by society and circumstances. Every chance we get to break free, we try, and sometimes get too tired and too hopeless to try yet again. When subdued for a long time, with no ray of hope, our survival instincts make us go silent, fearful of raising any more questions.

A small taste of courage, fantasy, dreams, and aspirations can kindle the courage gene. But half-baked courage can be detrimental too. Neither willing to accept the weakest social position in the hierarchy of my home nor having the courage to ask Amma directly, my forcibly restrained, unbound spirit brought the worst out of me. Unfortunately, I found this to be true for so many of us. Generation after generation, the stronger subdues the weaker, who passes it forward to the weaker still. And the cycle continues, be it the torment of women in developing countries or the fragile personalities at work in professional America.

My petite Pooja had offered the perfect antidote. While I waited for courage to show up, I used compassion to question the wrongdoing. Sometimes it is difficult to gather the courage to question for our own benefit, but often much easier to stand up for others. And in helping others, we also find the answers we seek.

Rituals

Be intentional about choosing your rituals.

The freedom to be ourselves makes us feel wholesome by taking us on a journey of self-discovery and growth. Consciously or subconsciously, we start following rituals that accelerate our journey or deviate from our path. Whether customary or habitual, rituals silently creep into our lives and govern us. Day after day, they leave ensuing marks to reshape our characters and redefine our beliefs.

Several of our conversations centered on our habits and rituals. Through open discussions, we become aware of them. These conversations played a crucial role in influencing us to write this book. And now, strive to be intentional about choosing those that propel us forward and abandon the ones that hold us back. We hope the following solo conversations will encourage you to do the same.

Nitya

Resurrect rituals to stay connected.

Growing up, life's cards seemed to play perpetual tricks on me and my sister. Our four-year age difference never let us collide in the same school. Despite this, sharing a room kept us close, giving us enough opportunities to bond. We were not just "sisters by chance" but also "friends by choice." That was until Didi (my elder sister) moved out for college, and we grew apart.

I entered high school with renewed hopes to find someone I could call "my best friend." Never had I imagined seeing our school's emotional counselor in that role. My mom often said that nobody is a horrible person, though everyone has quirks we must be aware of, which is why I was very confident in blindly pushing my narrative. "She's overall nice," I told the counselor. "We are friends. She made a mistake." I thought bullying ended with the elementary school "Don't be a bystander" workshops. Yet today I sat in his cold yet comforting chair, listening.

I had reached my tipping point. It had been a month of being followed around, threatened to being "exposed" (silly in hindsight, scary then), and called a "fake," undeserving of affection. Then, somewhere in the aftermath, suicide rumors about me circulated.

It had become a ritual to cry after every school day. Maybe everyone didn't know. Maybe everyone wasn't telling their group, "Don't tell anyone but I heard … about Nitya." But, perhaps, the most challenging part was accepting that somebody could hate me THIS much.

I had always considered myself a social person. As friendships became a game of hopscotch in school, despite jumping into many friend groups, I somehow made it to the inner circle. I tried, perhaps too hard, to be there for my friends. I was the friend who stayed on call when someone couldn't sleep, asked "how are you doing" every day - genuinely caring about the response, sent pep-talk texts before tests, and made care packages to pep someone up on their bad days.

As I alternated through the friend groups, the only thing that remained stable was my family. And today, I needed somebody- so to add to the oddities of the day, I reached out to the person seventy miles away. Didi, my elder sister.

A week later, the 2020 pandemic hit. Summer swung by and brought sophomore year along with it. Didi returned but now resided in the adjacent room; despite previously sharing a room for fourteen years.

I lay lethargic on my week-old sheets through day after day of online school. Naps and classes seasoned time as salt and pepper seasons a soggy subway sandwich. I stayed glued in my room, ignoring the world outside my bedroom walls. Occasionally, I peeped my head out for dinner and returned to my burrow to FaceTime my friends.

I was more comfortable communicating with school friends than family, a thought that sometimes became an uneasy feeling. It was fashionable for high schoolers to complain about family. I had always considered my mom and sister my friends and never understood the prevalent ritual behind asking – 'Are you close to your family?' Earlier, the answer seemed obvious – 'yes.' I mean, I live with them, see them every day. How could I NOT be close to my family? Yet, somewhere between my Mac screen and the confining bedroom walls, I was struggling for the answer now.

After the lull came the storm - Didi and I fought. Then we talked for a long while and cried. In the rehash of a new school and weakening family bonds, I had sought refuge outside in new friends. The issue is that when we approach friendships to replace our family, we cling to every Band-Aid we find.

As we stripped away the Band-Aid and sought to connect genuinely, we have resurrected family rituals. Through family Fridays, chats, and FaceTime, we started to make intentional efforts to stay connected. I'm truly grateful I now have friends within my family and a family of friends outside - those who held me tight when I was about to fall.

Naveli

Demolish rituals that hold us back.

As a little girl, I was always known to be happy. The girl who waved "Hi," to all the kids, parents, grandparents, and pets - taking thirty minutes to walk a quarter mile to elementary school. People called me a "butterfly" as I wandered in my wonderland.

This spell of happiness seems predestined to break. I was in middle school then. Walking home, I stopped on a bench near a park to take a sip of water. In the far corner, a boy twice my age was taunting a girl no older than me.

"You a sexy thing. Come home with me," I heard him slur.

"No! Get away. Leave me alone." Clawing at him, she ran away.

Her strength was evident. She left me wondering why such things happen, not just to the weak but also to the strong. Wasn't the world supposed to be a happy place?

A few months later, a strung-out forty-year-old man grabbed my arm at the mall and tried pulling me into him. I was with friends, just talking. A video of a girl dancing in her room in a tank top to Trap Queen by Fetty Wap circulated in high school. Many spoke about the video, suggestively commenting on her body. The school administration did nothing to stop them or the circulation of the video.

These incidents kept repeating like omnipresent rituals, some customary and others forming - from newspapers describing barbaric incidents in rural areas to cars full of boys honking at a group of girls simply walking to class in universities.

My happy-go-lucky outlook shifted. Though often a bystander, I experienced trauma in others and was gravely affected by the whimsical societal constructs that give way to rude, eerie behavior. As I studied the emergence of societal constructs, the reality of the world's occasionally destructive nature sunk in. Learnings of the Stanford Rape Case of 2014, Ted Bundy, and the Nirbhaya Rape Case of 2012 further helped me understand historical suppression.

Maturing and accepting the darker side of the world, I tried to block it from interfering with my forming identity. Continuously pondering, a pivotal question formed: Why do people do the things they do, whether good or bad? For example, how does someone decide to inflict harm or do well for another? In search of an answer, I turned to study the brain, specifically decision making. Recognizing intrinsic motivations (why one does something) can help us understand the extrinsic frameworks that govern us (the societal constructs we fit ourselves into).

Flashbacks to the park girl led me to a Women Studies class. Intrigued by the duality of vulnerability and femininity in the patriarchy, I wondered how learned societal behaviors had shaped us. Though a rude awakening, I found comfort in cognizing the stigma surrounding women empowerment. Not only do adverse events directly correlate to the brain's health, even the aftermath of divulging the trauma can halter our thoughts from progressing. For instance, rape culture and victim-blaming are known to silence the survivors, a conscious societal decision.

Through numerous life stories and neuroscience classes, I learned how lasting scars from repressive rituals preclude us from living a wholesome life. Yet, little to no research approaches the intersection of women-specific hardships and oppression with brain development and decision-making skills.

I aim to understand, devalue, and break societal stigmas around trauma through a scientific lens. We may not be able to eliminate all trauma. But, armed with such knowledge, we can demolish the rituals prohibiting generations from staying blissfully happy and avoid forcing them towards distressful awareness as they enter adulthood. Somewhere there is also my path back to the ever-happy girl I was born to be.

Manisha

Create rituals that make us feel wholesome.

Every night I would hold her hand and ask, "Are you at peace?" Every night she would extend the other hand, a cue to help her get up. We would climb the stairs, hug each other good night, and move into our respective rooms to sleep.

A week had passed. I was to fly back the next day. The sun was finally out, filling the family room with bright rays pouring in from the life-size window.

We had been exchanging childhood memories all afternoon. Shalu Didi, my husband's cousin, fondly remembered and vividly elaborated on her childhood days. An army of maids at her disposal - massaging her hair, adorning her hands with henna. She referred to her mother as "my soulmate" as she narrated the story of the two characters flawlessly executing their covert mission to have Didi participate in a beauty pageant. Unfortunately busted by newspaper headlines declaring Shalu Didi as Ms. Ajmer. Her dramatics were in full swing as she animated how they had pleaded guilty and rolled out in laughter the moment they had the room.

She was still beautiful. Still lively.

Shalu Didi had wanted to stay in her hometown. However, grandiose dreams of her soul mate mother saw her marrying into a reputed family and moving to the USA. Rituals transitioned the princess into a perfect cook, a perfect maid, a perfectly silent wife, and a regular pay stub and insurance provider.

She had wanted kids. "I love dressing up, and dressing girls up," she had chuckled, lying on that couch staring at the wieldy bamboo plant stationed on the right edge of the partition wall.

My eyes, glued on the tea pan, glanced at her. The bamboo and Didi aligned in one straight line, their strength concealed behind their untimely wrinkles.

I watered the plant. We drank the tea in silence. Then, passing the cup back, in the usual "I don't want to disturb anyone" manner, Didi whispered that her eyes were burning. I dipped two cotton balls in freshly squeezed cucumber juice and signaled her to lay her head on my lap. A few minutes later, she slept - her face calm as the cucumber juice relaxed her eyes, and I pressed her head.

I was meditating in the faint rhythms of her heartbeat when she proclaimed, "Today, I feel wholesome."

"Why just today?" my eyes quizzed her. "Why not every day?" Remembering the mark their family had made in Ajmer, I urged, "Would you like me to record your stories? Narrate. I will write." Her eyes twinkled; she nodded then quickly corrected, "He (her husband) may not approve." She was right.

We used to call Shalu Didi's mom "Pyaari Maa," who indeed lived up to that name, lovingly taking care of everything for everyone. Maybe so much that Didi never learned self-care.

All the talking had visibly tired her. She wanted to retire to bed early. So, I ritually held her hand and repeated yet again, "Are you at peace?"

I realized that my eyes had given away more than I had wanted as she spelled out loud, "In case I don't wake up?" and indulged, "Yes I am at peace. I forgive everyone."

Our hug was firm and long that night. Then, as we disentangled from each other, years of restless hopes and fears transferred from one body to another, making her stories an integral part of my being. I could not sleep that night, not sure if I was right in expecting her to be at peace.

A few days later, she texted, "I am in the hospital. At peace," and succumbed to cancer, a disease known to thrive under chronic stress, leaving me to wonder if things might have been different if we had created rituals that made her feel wholesome every day.

Words Matter

Our thoughts become our reality.

Naveli

Dirty Dishes

"Naveli & Nitya, when are the dirty dishes in your room planning to come to the sink?" We heard Mom's voice from the kitchen.

"I was about to put them down," I answered without lifting my head.

"No, those words carry no meaning," Mom was now standing at the door of my room. "You know that, and I know that."

"I will do it," Nitya chimed in.

"Then do it now. And put them in the dishwasher." Mom was persistent.

She collected the dishes from our study tables and nightstands and handed them to both of us. Her body language quite clear about the urgency of the situation. So, we did.

We came back to our room to find Mom folding our clothes. "Mom, it's okay. We will do it," I assured her.

"If you are saying it, mean it."

"Words matter," Nitya nodded.

"Whether I think I can or I can't, I am right," I chimed in. We smiled at each other. And having conveyed that we understood each other, we dispersed into our respective lives again.

Mantras

Crisp air blew into my bedroom through the open window, filling the room with an air of freshness. The day was bright. In the distance, I heard a flock of birds chirp, signaling it was wake-up time. As I pulled my blanket closer to me, I felt the warmth of my bed, making me less inclined to leave.

Then, I heard my Dadaji chanting, "OooHhhhMmmmmmmmm." My cue. So I sat up, stretched, and climbed down from the top bunk bed.

I heard phrases like *Ohm* often. *OHM* is the primordial sound, I was told. A vibration. A sensation. Even our Wi-Fi was named OHM. Whether during *poojas* in the morning or as a greeting, chants and mantras constantly reminded us that words could bring happiness and tranquility and were effective mood transformers.

I found comfort in mantras as I did in songs and some sayings. The chorus of One Direction's "Diana" or the Hindi song "Luka Chuppi" from the movie *Rang De Basanti*. Mumma's rendition of the "Nanhi Kali sone chali" lullaby. My internal monologue of "Breathe. Just Breathe." These words powered me through my day.

Mom was always insistent on not using strong words, especially the negative ones. No sooner had the words "I *hate* this chapter" come out of my mouth than she was quick to correct, "You *dislike* it." BEST friends became GOOD friends. "Words matter," she would often say, "Thoughts matter; they become our reality."

And yet she was the one who broke her own rule. I remember the feeling exceptionally well, though the day has now muddled in my memory. I must have been about fourteen years old then. The word had been uttered previously on many occasions. But this became the first of a long road that hurt me time and time again.

Mumma and I were arguing about something to do with my actions that day. I had tried to justify my behavior, stating that I felt a certain way. In response, Mom said, "Stop this victim behavior."

I retaliated. "I'm not. I'm explaining my side."

"You're victimizing yourself. Just own up to your mistakes gracefully. And don't do it again."

The following argument happened maybe two days later. It was most probably regarding my bad habit of leaving dishes littered around the house. And again, there was that word. *Victim.*

I was aware of my highly empathetic personality and tendency to overthink. So, I tried not to be impacted by it or internalize it. But the more I wanted to stop it, the more it stuck.

A few months later, we had another argument. And even before Mom said the word, my internal mantra repeated the phrases back to me. *Stop victimizing. You are a victim. Are you a victim? Stop victimizing.* I was upset, almost furious by now.

And she repeated it, "Why do you believe you are a victim, Navi?"

I was done. I had to say something to stop it. "I am not a victim. Just hear me out. And stop saying that! That isn't ME," I yelled back.

"Then why are you yelling?" Her voice also raised a bit.

I took a deep breath, lowered my volume, and stared straight at her. "Me explaining what I was thinking or doing isn't me saying 'pity me.' Or that life is too difficult for me. It isn't me saying 'poor me' at all. It's me trying to have a conversation and tell you what I am thinking. It's me somewhere defending my actions. Trying to help you understand my actions."

"Okay, but you are somewhere victimizing. Even if you don't mean to pity yourself, you are talking with that emotion. Maybe not intentionally, but you are doing it," she responded.

"You calling me a victim is you convincing yourself that everything I am saying is with that intent in mind. It makes you feel that you have the upper hand, the power. And that dealing with me in this way is okay. But that's not okay."

By then, the word *victim* was a negative internal mantra, and it coming out of her mouth was an unforgivable crime. That argument-turned-conversation was the first time I called Mumma out on her word choices. But, unfortunately, the effect of that word on me hadn't sunk in for her.

Like most households with growing kids, our arguments, misunderstandings, and fights were rampant. I felt this irk against Mumma, whether it was our generational gaps, cultural differences, or simply being the oldest child and the family's parenting guinea pig. She ended up being the one I fought with more than the rest.

Junior year of high school brought its own set of challenges. The pressures were rising on all ends - academically, socially, and emotionally. Nothing was routine about that day, nor had the week felt right. Yet I tried to stick to my schedule - after school, take the bus, get off, get picked up by Mom.

"How was your day?" she asked her usual question.

"Fine." Dry, I didn't care to answer the question. My head was spinning.

"You look off," Mumma noted.

I didn't know what to say. And as I sat with the sun shining over my sullen face, I thought, *What's the worst that could happen if I tell her?* So, I did.

That night, I sat in our Chevy Volt– a car that would later become mine– and told Mom about everything that happened. The intoxication. The assault. The fallout. Cyberbullying. Tears flew out of our eyes. Mom's face changed from being shocked to confused to hurt as words strangled to come out of my throat. Then, thirsty, we got out of the car after three hours of reaching home to sip water.

Inside, the conversation ensued. Mom seemed angry. "How did you let yourself fall victim to all this?"

All I heard was the word. *Victim.*

At this point, no, we were not just conversing. At this point, we were straight-up fighting. Hurt, anger, and thousands of other emotions in the air, I became furious and lashed out. "YOU WERE THE ONE THAT TOLD ME TO NEVER BE A *BICHARI* (pity worthy), MOM. THEN, WHY DO YOU KEEP TELLING ME THAT I'M ACTING LIKE A VICTIM?"

That ended the fight.

Mom later explained the growth versus victim mindset theory. She continuously asked me why that word hurt me so much for the next few years. I didn't fully understand and couldn't articulate. But, somewhere, I was triggered by it. Perhaps another reason why I pursued psychology some two years later a college.

And yet the word 'pity' didn't hurt me at all. Mom and I talked about this too. "What word is okay to use then, Navi? When I want to tell you that you are being emotional about a topic and inflicting pain on yourself. What word should I use then? ... How about pity?"

"That's fine. Though I don't pity myself."

Naveli's Diary

As I dive deeper into neuroscience and psychology at university, I understand the social repercussions of language and its interconnection with human emotions.

As Piaget noted, kids in both the concrete (7-11 years) and formal (11+) operational stages see changes in how they experience self-esteem intertwined with language. Stemming from the fact that kids at these ages spend a lot of time with their peers, social relations and meaningful connections are therefore necessary for their self-identity. Discourse with a professor helped me understand how communication and language are the roots of these connections. And how the words become defining points in our lives. We see them as labels. Unfortunately, labels can hurt as much as they can heal.

*Words do matter. As much as the word victim paralyzed me, the concept of "not everyone is a **best** friend" helped me nurture meaningful friendships. I learned to prepare to say, "Already done" and get over my habit of saying "Almost done." Hate became dislike, and many more such changes have become so deeply embedded in my psychology that I find them hard to remember now.*

Even now, as I come back from college with new slang and verbiage, she reminds me of the importance of choosing the right words. Most recently, my habit of constantly saying, "Not going to lie" met with the spy in my mom. "So, are you generally lying? Why else do you specify that you aren't lying?"

Our words become us. And the impact of our words on others can last a lifetime. I still try to follow our family rule of "No strong words" in my day-to-day life.

Nitya's Diary

It seems to me that my generation romanticizes victimizing ourselves. Everyone seems to expect us to enjoy the pleasantries of our privileged lives. Yet it has started to feel that our generation feels obligated to smother ourselves in manufactured issues first. At least, the mentality at my school has become such. We don't think that we are doing enough unless we also feel the suffering from doing so.

For the first time in middle school, I learned what the word optimism meant when leadership students addressed the subject as a mini lesson. It sounded friendly and straightforward; if you choose to appreciate the positives in life rather than dwell on the negatives, your life will suddenly seem a lot better. The challenging part was putting it into practice, but I was determined to try. The next day, I thought about what an optimistic mindset and a pessimistic mindset would say about events throughout my day. My friends noted that my nature was generally to see the positive. Still, there were times when I dwelled in negativity unnecessarily. So, over the next year, I grew to play this game with myself. A simple way to make life happier.

In high school, my mindset significantly improved. But reflecting on myself had allowed me to realize how many of my friends tended to use strong words to justify negative emotions. For example, after arguing with a parent over their grades in school, one might say, "my parents hate me." I would repeat, "Hate you? They don't hate you, they're just mad right now, but that's because they care." Some students might consider themselves lucky to have parents who care. Still, in this case, the conclusion was reached as my friend strongly asserted their claim; their parents hated them.

This phenomenon became evident when my AP Psychology teacher pointed out how we one-up each other with miscommunication. For example, students compete to claim they lost more sleep than others as they stayed up working. There is subtle competition also in victimizing themselves from their parents. Finally, there is a pride in, simply put, who lives a shittier life. And in this thirst to win, we exaggerate and extreme our pains to match others. Silencing the voices of those genuinely aching.

The worst example I saw was when a friend was sexually abused recently. In response, our mutual friends shared their stories from when they were younger. While they had no intention of doing so, unknowingly, they started to "one-up" the friend's pain instead of offering solace.

Everyone's story is their own, but by heightening our stories with strong words to match or compete with others, we create unexpected consequences. It's worth living with an optimistic mindset instead, even if it comes with the hassle of watching our words and tailoring them to the situation, not exaggerating it.

Manisha

The vibrations in their sounds carry the power to weigh us down or blow air beneath our wings. A childhood story I read back in India was titled "Vani ka Vardan" (The blessings of speech). The fictional story took us back to the beginning of time. It was said that humans had lived for centuries peacefully. Then aspirations grew - to settle down from a nomadic life and communicate better. They prayed for years and wished for the gods to give them a voice. Gods hesitated. Debated. Then agreed, and the voice transcended down to Earth.

Humans had already established numerous ways to express love, affection, and emotions with hugs, kisses, pats on the back, smiles, and cheers. But to express anger, they could only growl or walk away in disgust. The voice now offered an equitable ground to represent both emotions. So, good words and foul words were created. Communication improved, and conversations started flowing; languages were formed. Structured communication took shape, cities, governments, and societies were developed, and books were authored. But disputes, mistrust, deceits, and boundaries also grew as the words made it easy to express and grow negative emotions.

Our Hindi teacher had savvily ended the story with a question - "Why had the gods hesitated? Was Vani (Voice) indeed a *vardan* (blessing) or, in fact, an *abhishaap* (curse)?" The words used in the follow-up discussion in that elementary school classroom steered our young minds to use these expensive words wisely.

Emotions take over all of us. They make us enter the spirals of self-criticism or delve into criticizing people who think differently than us. To save us from falling into such traps, we have planted quotes all over our house. But, of course, they work only 90% of the time. We also developed a habit of expressing care through words and gestures. Often saying aloud, "I love you," is also a reminder for us as it is a message for others. Words also have the power to create trust.

Vedic scriptures cite numerous stories of nonverbal communication through mental vibration of thoughts and expressions. Words were succinct and occasionally used.

Our world relies heavily on words, be it written or spoken. We connect words to trust or doubt at a very young age. Kids have been good at keeping me honest since they were in elementary school. When I had failed to put up the Christmas tree after repeatedly saying, "We will put up the tree tonight," the lack of trust in my words was visible in their eyes. So I learned to pick up the phone and book a slot before committing to making a dash to Michaels to pick up art supplies. Since then, we have created family group chats and calendars to stay connected and transparent with each other.

When our words conflict with our actions, they create a deceiving perception of us and make us look fake and untrustworthy.

When we say something, we must mean it and act on it. Yet, being mortal humans, we get tempted to slip and slide away from the words we once said. Just acknowledging this and giving space to a trustworthy person when they occasionally falter, we can offer a chance for them to self-reflect and self-correct, thus maturing us and our relationship.

Having convinced the gods, it's up to each of us individually to use our voice as a blessing or as a curse.

Two-way Street

Dots connect with a single line; people connect on a two-way street.

Nitya

The Kiddie Jar

I watched this show the other day where a mom implemented a swear jar. The kid had to pay a quarter every time they uttered foul words. Later, this concept of teaching was questioned, questioning the merit of punishments and rewards without explanation.

I think it is a familiar feeling for most kids. Our curious minds are advised to abide obediently by adult instructions and against trying to grow up too fast if we continue questioning them. It's still unknown if this was my imagination or the truth, but being belittled constantly as the kid in the family had started to hurt significantly as I grew older.

In my sophomore year, I opened to Dad about my feelings - about him treating me like a kid and sarcastically commenting, "I was trying to grow up too fast." As a precursor to our talk, Mom and I had openly discussed the situation and my feelings. While I accepted I was a kid, she also admitted that I was mature in many aspects.

To the outside world, my teachers, aunts, uncles, and my friend's parents have noted me as being mature for my age. For example, during Diwali, the Indian festival of lights, just a few weeks before my chat with Dad, Didi and I went to drop off *mithai*, Indian sweets, in the neighborhood and to our teachers. A few minutes into the conversation at my old art teacher's house, she said, "Both of you look so grown-up but yeah, this one I know; she's always been quite mature for her age." Besides art, I also danced, sang, and debated at school. I was also in Leadership. Teachers always seemed to tell me how developed and mature my thoughts were throughout these creative outlets.

I suppose that what hurt was the family, who was supposed to know me super well, was treating me like I was just the youngest.

With Didi, it made sense; I mean, what I saw was an older sister who wanted to look out for her younger one. Sure, sometimes she would baby me, and it bothered me, but most of the time, I was able to let it go.

Mom measured my maturity based on my thoughts rather than the number of years I had been on this earth. She used to often say that exposure makes a person. She strived to provide us with new experiences and opportunities. Sometimes I would walk in willingly into the gates she opened; other times, she would push me in. But she was around when I needed her. Or a text away. And we often had intellectual conversations along with trivial ones.

Those mature aspects being overlooked by Dad felt wrong. I was trying too hard to grow up, but only because being the "youngest" had become an absolute status in Dad's eyes. I understand that we will always remain a kid in our parents' eyes. When you take on adult responsibilities and get a kid's credit, it feels as if nothing is ever enough to make them see you as anything more than a kid. The feeling sticks within. And the feeling starts hurting. Maybe it was imagination. But then, our hallucinations only extend from what we know to be true.

But obviously, none of this is cut and dry, nor was his behavior pervasive. With Dad, it was a little different when I was actually young. I cleared the ATP (Advanced Talent) program. This program was offered in a school further away from our home. So, we used to carpool. During Dad's turns, he would quiz us and joke with us. As little kids, we were excited to learn new things. We didn't always blindly follow along, but questioning and correcting Dad generally ended on amicable terms. He would accept, "Oops, I was wrong, good job," laugh, and move on.

Unfortunately, that unraveled as I grew up. Slowly the amicable questioning between Dad and daughter was labeled as "my constant need to argue with him." Or so it felt.

In my eyes, I came to Dad, excited with new information that I had just researched that might augment or contradict his own findings. But instead, I was told to stop arguing. At that age, tearing my point down only brought me back up stronger as I was too naive to let it go and too adamant about being right, just as my dad was. So, over time, these small, seemingly harmless fights created giant craters between us, and his view of me was plastered with the word "argumentative."

Over many conversations with Mom, we agreed that some relations are always to be nurtured. But in a way that makes everyone feel heard and belong. I think Mom and Didi discussed this with Dad also. We took the opportunity that shelter at home had offered to plan family discussions. Initially, Dad and I would argue and, at times, walk away. But Mom reminded us, "Argument is to prove who is right, discussion to understand what is right." And I started using that as a mantra.

With continued efforts, we started listening and accepting. Now I feel confident that I can question Dad, but respectfully. I understand that he is open to understanding my point even if we contradict. And I feel close to him again.

Manisha

Are we really talking?

Alone, Nitya and I could both talk fast and understand each other without finishing the sentence. Our conversations were all over the map, as were our experiments. These dates could be anything - spas, bookstores, shopping, ice cream walks. The point was to spend time together while catching up with each other.

As Nitya entered high school, dates disappeared from our calendars. Our patience also declined, and we started snapping at each other. Her affinity for friends rose, and as Naveli moved back to college in Davis, their connection conversely loosened.

One day, I saw Nitya entering the house; she was back from school.

Hours passed by as we both completed our own work inside our rooms. After many giggles and animations from her room that day, I heard a moment of silence. A second later, she appeared in my home office. She leaned closer as I sat buried in my laptop. Then announced, "For our next assignment, we are supposed to create a dance piece addressing a meaningful societal topic. Any ideas?"

I inquired, "What did you discuss with your team?"

"Well, we discussed a few ideas - drugs, depression, body shaming. School has a lot of such things going on these days," she responded.

"Okay, so where did you land?" I continued.

She paused, then added, "That is the thing; all these seem fake. As if we are doing something for the heck of doing it because everyone is."

"But not something you can relate with. Not meaningful for you," I confirmed my understanding, to which Nitya nodded.

"Have you considered why schools suffer from these things so much?" I asked. She looked up as I continued, "Four of you just spent an hour talking to each other. But were you really talking? Do you know what is going on in each other's lives? Where might you be able to help meaningfully?"

She walked back to her room, and I immersed myself back in my laptop.

The next day I received a text from Nitya. "Mom, we have finalized our topic. 'When we talk, let's really talk.' We will prepare a medley where each of us will express through dance what is really going on in our minds and our lives."

"Great," I responded.

"Thank you," she replied.

After a few minutes, I received another text, "And can we plan our date again?"

"Of course," I texted back, smiling.

"And yes, when we talk, let's really talk," she responded back with many emojis.

Nitya's Diary

Meaningful conversations and connections are a two-way street.

Naveli

The Birthday Gift

I struggled with interconnectedness in the family quite a bit while growing up. Fights were frequent. We simply couldn't escape them initially, though as we matured, the frequency decreased.

A random day has solidified in my memory. I was in fifth and Nitya in first. Our bunk beds were separated in our lilac room. Lilac was my favorite color, and "N" was my letter -they defined me. The idea that Nitya shared both was not sitting well those days.

We had the quintessential fight siblings indulge in all over the Bay. Our problem: clothes. Though it sounds uber materialistic on the surface, it wasn't about clothes. Instead, it was about the principle of shared items. Much like my earlier memories of my childhood, I can't remember what the fight was precisely about, barring some key moments. Around 6:00 p.m., as the sun was setting, conversations between Nitya and me started escalating into a war. I remember running around the house screaming, "No, this is mine. You can't claim it. It is my birthday gift and it's still new. What made you think you could wear it to school today? Without even asking me?"

Unsurprisingly, she responded, "It's both of ours. We share a closet. Why don't you understand that?" We were back in our room, pacing, when she halted to slide open the closet's right side, her side.

I paused, "Yes. No, but .. not this." I was hurt. *Why was there no boundary for her?* I thought. My voice wavered. *Inhale, exhale, deep breaths ....* my eyes watering, I lowered my voice. "Because this one is mine. And yet you wore it today with no respect for me."

124

Mad, she raised her voice, "Didi, why do you always make it about you? Let me be."

Angry, I stormed over to the closet, ripping it open to expose my side of the cabinet, "Take anything else." I didn't notice how angry I was, and in my rage, I slid the closet hard. The door went screeching through her fingers as she held onto the closet wall on the other end. I felt bad. But my first reaction? "Oh my god, oh my god. Don't tell Mumma. After all, this was your fault."

Years later, that agonizing screech still rings in my ears.

That fight might've been one of the most brutal between us. And so, it was always a topic that came back again and again in every conflict that followed. It took many years to realize that the fault was mine. That I needed to make amends.

The more I understood Nitya, the more I learned that it wasn't about clothes for her that day. Nitya and I have talked about this openly, that Nitya had started hating me at one point. Correction - she had started intensely disliking some of my actions.

She told me how somewhere, maybe she was jealous of me. She had started feeling like she wasn't enough. She thought I was prettier, better dressed, and better understood, while she felt belittled. Maybe she wanted to feel like her perception of me by wearing that dress.

She helped me too. Through understanding her and then other people, I began to understand myself. An innate feeling, I, too, had a habit of comparing myself to others. I used to feel that people judged me when maybe they didn't. The hold that others had over me impacted my empathy, emotions, and anger. It became effortless to simply assume the worst. I used to catch myself thinking that way sometimes. Dad's voice echoed in my brain. *Assuming makes an ass out of you and me.*

In one of our family conversations, we identified each other's strengths and opportunities for improvement. Now we lean on each other to round up our sharp edges. Simply talking to Nitya, and my family, helped me understand how to deal with the world and with myself.

Courage

Grow confidence in your actions and thoughts.

Self-Doubt

Master the mind before the mind masters you.

Nitya

The Pink Cape

There's this fear in school: the fear of being alone. For me, it started in middle school. Girls piled up in bathrooms, entering and exiting with their entourages. When somebody has to go to the bathroom, they don't just go; they ask their group to accompany them. Nobody says it, but nobody wants to be caught walking alone.

I started high school. Though it's implausible that everyone is watching you with a class size of seven hundred and a school population of four thousand, we still believe that they do. And If we walk out of a building alone, we might be judged for lack of friends.

I was friends with many individuals, each of whom I connected with. But each of them was part of a different friend group, and I had none. So, as I started the new school, I tried being part of one. So, I embraced a new friendship: a short, thick, curly-haired, loud, extroverted girl. In her friend group was another girl - long straight hair, medium height, quieter. She had opinions but was more conscious and careful in her actions. Lunchtimes with this friend group were fun, but I became quieter despite my extroverted personality. And then I realized. The curly-haired girl sucked away all the attention, often the only one that spoke. In contrast, others had become followers, I included.

So, I willfully left the friend group to be stranded alone again. The curly hair girl tried all sorts of tactics to humiliate me. I was steadfast. Then after being publicly humiliated, when I saw an old friend, I ran crying to her and told the whole story. All my old friends, true friends scattered through multiple groups, helped me gain strength. And though they returned to their separate circles for lunchtime and bathroom breaks, I didn't feel lonely anymore.

I walked down the halls alone. Confident that right behind me were those true friends and my family. And most importantly, guarding me was my ability to stand up for what felt right.

Then I found someone like me, standing tall alone, Rani, now a close friend. And over the years, I have met many such friends who choose to retain their identity and accept their differences, sometimes even celebrating them.

A girl a year older than me was pretty well-known at school for dancing. However, her larger frame and broader shoulders made her body look nothing like a typical dancer. Yet, she carried herself with grace and confidence. She never let her insecurities show publicly. Instead, she wrote her own narrative, and others just watched and listened.

I also realized somebody right under my nose had also learned to befriend herself and conquer her self-doubt. Didi had formed a Bollywood dancing club at her predominantly American school. She was the only Indian girl in the club, and through her passion and confidence, she had made Bollywood a source of joy and bonding for many in her school. She called the dance club Athenian Awaaz. A more traditional name might have been Athenian Andaaz. But while "andaaz" means style, "awaaz" means voice. She created the club to become a voice, and I aspired to do the same. And I found it finally with the help of a pink cape.

Most schools have spirit days when students deck out in color or for a theme to show their pride in being part of their school's community. Unfortunately, while my school, Dougherty Valley, thrived in studies, the academic excellence came at the cost of students prioritizing funnier aspects of the school atmosphere, including spirit days.

Kids in the leadership club are expected to promote school spirit. But in our school, even leadership kids were embarrassed to dress up in unusual attires. Personally, I enjoyed dressing up for most spirit days, time permitting. So, I often dressed up, but not to a noticeable extent.

This spirit day was celebrated at school and at the football game to promote breast cancer awareness. We had lost a dear one to breast cancer in our family, so this one mattered to me more. And so that day, I decided not only to dress pink but also to make an impression on others. I came to school in a pink cropped shirt with a mini looped pink ribbon pinned to it, jeans with a pink makeshift silk ribbon belt, two small braids with pink beads in my straightened hair, two pink Mardi Gras necklaces around my neck, pink friendship bracelets on my wrist, a pink bandana tied to my leg, pink eyeshadow on my eyelids, and a grand flowing pink cape. If I had faked my confidence and was awkward about my outfit, people would've made jokes - even if they were lighthearted. But instead, I was proud of my attire, and it showed so much so that others asked to borrow my cape and my Mardi Gras beads; others wanted to become a part of a greater cause with me. And so, after school, by the time of the football game, I had influenced about a dozen friends to join me in dressing up in pink to spread breast cancer awareness.

The more I befriended myself, the more my confidence grew. As a district head came in one day and asked us to voice concerns on problems they could help fix, I was among the first to raise my hand. In the past, when vulnerable was my fear, now I found strength in embracing my vulnerability. As I voiced my story, others chimed in, sharing their own stories. Voices piled one on top of another until the wellness center was created a few months later. Students go daily to destress by vocalizing their stories, overcoming their self-doubts, and finding their best friend hidden somewhere within.

Nitya's Diary

I learned that I will never learn to lead if I follow blindly, and If I seek a change, I must ask for a change, whether within my family, school, or peers. But for me to lead and to ask, I have to start with becoming my own friend first.

Naveli

Chemistry

Some conversations we need to have simply with ourselves. Understanding and identifying who we are and what we want to be. These conversations often are the beginnings of long-winded roads that don't end. They repeatedly loop, causing confusion, inviting reconsideration, and sometimes a self-wallowing doubt. Self-doubt.

High school is supposed to be a time of self-growth and discovery, with counsel from parents, teachers, and counselors. I had all that. Still, on and off, I fell into the self-doubting trap. Circling.

Up until eighth grade, I was in public school. I had tried to stay on top of my North Pole and truly believed I was on a good path. But my parents didn't think alike. So, in June 2015, as I was "*promoted*" to high school, I joined summer courses in a private school to get ahead in my science and math requirements.

Unfortunately, my definition of being "on top" was not aligned with my parents' ideas. I would try to be on top of my assignments, especially long-lasting projects, but ultimately, I would procrastinate. In addition, the ZAP from sixth grade hadn't made as much of a mark as I thought it did. Finally, Mom researched that the private school's structure and one-on-one attention might help me get realigned. Dad agreed.

One late night in August changed my fate. I attended Dougherty Valley High School for two days, convinced that my future lay in its beautiful grounds with all my friends. But though I put up a good fight, Mom and Dad ultimately convinced me to move to a private school to help me stay focused. I know I am privileged to be able to make such choices. Still, I wasn't happy.

In a turn of events, I somehow started blossoming at Quarry Lane. The richer experiences in the dance and theater departments sparked new ideas. I experimented with Computer Science, influenced by my computer-savvy parents. I boomeranged academically and was engaged at all levels at school. I made friends, founded clubs, and connected my old networks with new ones to make Quarry Lane visible in the Bay Area school circles.

But there was one setback. Chemistry. In ninth grade, I took Honors Chemistry with Dr. K. According to my seniors, Dr. K was "the best teacher ever" and would make chemistry "my favorite subject." So naturally, I was ecstatic. So, at the beginning of the school year in September, I went into the class extremely excited.

The school year started with the basic overviews of measurements and conversions, lab procedures, and safety. The same routine overviews that we do in every science class. We were gearing up for stoichiometry. And then... sometime in October, Dr. K left Quarry Lane. Abruptly. Leaving us students bewildered. Who would teach? What now...?

For the next six-seven weeks, Quarry Lane provided us with multiple substitute teachers at the pace of one sub per week. None of them, unfortunately, were well versed in teaching chemistry. So, we would sit for long hours listening to the subs trying to explain stoichiometry, but nothing made sense. My confidence in the subject dropped as every new sub added to the already brewing confusion.

Then finally, the week before Thanksgiving break, Quarry Lane hired Dr. W, an academic with similar credentials to Dr. K and in-depth chemistry background. He came in believing we had covered the syllabus and announced semester finals within a week of his joining. We all freaked. My confidence was now at rock bottom.

Out came Sai, a student and a friend who understood chemistry and was willing to teach us. During the break, we had group sessions where he would teach and quiz us on the material. After the pause, we confessed to Dr. W. that we hadn't learned much through the subs and instead learned from Sai. Bewildered but understanding, he decided to only test us on the first few chapters of information instead of half of the textbook. And a semester from hell was finally over.

Then came January. With a confident jolt of energy, Dr. W was determined to teach the entire high school chemistry in this one semester. So, we began the journey of cramming more than a chapter of the textbook every week for the next fifteen weeks. And though I understood part of the concepts, I became hung up on stoichiometry. The conversions. Moles. Limiting reagents. Molar mass. Everything juggled in my head to find meaning.

I started gearing up for the final in May, but I didn't feel confident. "Chemistry was not for me," I told my parents. My mom listened intently. She was in her last semester at Wharton too. Stressed out and spread thin already, the stress of me struggling in chemistry weighed on her the most. Determined, she took on the mission to make sure I studied and did well in the class. But self-doubt had wrapped itself around my neck like a snake, tightening its grip every time I thought about chemistry. So, I wrote it off and stopped thinking about it. The more I appeared blocked, the more motivated Mom seemed to make me get over my block.

See, I'm pretty stubborn when I want to be. So, my catch-phrase– *Whether you think you can or you think you can't, you're always right* – was spot on. But unfortunately, this time to my detriment. I had developed what Mom called a block, a mental hindrance that persists even when one is succeeding at something, inevitably halting the progress in said goal.

Mom grappled with my self-doubt and stoichiometry for the next month, along with her full-time job, housework, and finishing up her MBA. I didn't understand it at the time, the effort she was putting into me. The unwavering belief she had in me. Instead, it felt like nagging, and I ached for it to stop.

After countless late nights, the material started making sense, but "stoich" was still a block. Then we devised a plan with just a few days to go for my finals. Mumma had to go for a Wharton global learning course in Rwanda, where her days were packed. During her thirty hours long flight time, she studied the remaining concepts of stoichiometry. She made notes, and, at every layover, she emailed her cliff notes and taught me over a Wi-Fi connection.

With wavering confidence, I took the final. I passed with a good grade and credited it all to one-time luck.

For reasons not relevant to this conversation, the summer after sophomore year, I again switched schools to join a holistic private school, The Athenian School, located at the base of Mount Diablo. It emphasized arts as much as science and provided the environment I needed to blossom in my own way. As a result, I developed a love for biology, calculus, and random bits of English. But all along, I kept telling myself that I *hated* chemistry. To the point where the moment we did even the tiniest bit of biochemistry in biology, my block would make me lean on my peers. And yet, I led the dissections, anatomy, and physiology, which excited me.

Oscillating between my varied life experiences, I developed a liking to study the human brain. An internship with VISIONS helped vet out the possibility of clinical psychology as a career option of my liking. Research eventually led to a major in Neurobiology, Physiology, and Behavior (NPB). The perfect culmination of psychology, anatomy, and research. Then the realization hit. Chemistry. Not just one but three courses of general chemistry. And not just general chemistry but also a series of organic chemistry.

I did well in the first general chemistry class – CHE 2A– but the block kept visiting. Determined to overcome it, I tried my best. But froze and failed the course giving into the cognitive dissonance that ninth-grade chemistry was a stroke of one-time luck.

I retook the class. Stoichiometry somehow clicked within a few weeks, making me feel stupid. It was so easy. I couldn't understand what had grappled me for the past four years. This gave me some hope. I just had to stay committed.

Hope has a characteristic. It grows. If I could understand such a crucial subject, perhaps I could do medical school too. Convinced that neuroscience research was my calling, I validated my thinking with several neuroscientists and doctors. I switched majors. Then slowly made my way through the three general chemistry courses, each giving me some kind of hurdle. Due to the pandemic, the online second gen chem class posed additional challenges of understanding labs through TA-led videos instead of hands-on experience. I took the third class in a six-week fast-paced summer session to catch up with the new major. Also, fully online.

In-person instructions were back by Junior year. It was time for the first of the Organic Chemistry trio, who was said to be the most challenging professor in the chemistry department. How much of that is true, I do not know. But those words left an impression and offered self-doubt a chance to settle in again. Nevertheless, I was determined to consciously push through the block. I attended numerous study sessions, got a tutor, and read the textbook ahead of time. I tried. Yet, I didn't do well in midterm one.

The snake around my neck tightened its grip once again. But I kept pushing through. Midterm two went much better. Still, I was unsure. So, I continued feeding the antidote, perseverance. The untimely introduction of a complex synthesis concept in the last week of class shook many of my classmates. The class revolted to no avail. I studied as much as possible and took the finals. And I passed. Earlier, I had hoped to do better, but I was happy to successfully pull through with all my zest.

For five years now, I have been self-doubting my abilities in chemistry. I have to take the second Organic Chemistry class in the summer. Somewhere, I am dreading it. But somewhere, I know that I can and will succeed at it.

December 2021 was a big decision-making month for me. Repetitive bouts of self-doubt leave us feeling lonely even after trying our best. Giving my all and still feeling like I was failing tore away at me.

The emotions swirled in my head. Moving on with neuroscience meant more chemistry ahead. I could push through, but was it worth it? When I had the option to pursue options, that made me do more out of excitement, not fear. I could voice it out, but first, I had to confront my feelings and decide before sharing them with my family, who had been with me literally every step.

My blocks have held my life in contempt. Yet, conversations with myself led to continuous little realizations to continue confronting self-doubts and steering in the direction where the winds will help me fly towards my aspirations and dreams.

Fearlessly. Block free.

Manisha

A big fat zero.

It was the summer of 2015. As I entered the house through the garage door, I could sense a feeling of annoyance flowing within me upon noticing the dark alleys followed by the dark rooms. Nobody had cared to turn the lights on.

But where was everybody? I walked up the stairs to the kid's room. Naveli seemed upset, lying on her bed. "How was your day?" I asked.

"Okay," came the telegraphic answer.

"What is wrong?" I enquired casually.

"Nothing."

"Can we talk?" I asked. My emotions intermingled between irritability and concern as I stood trapped in my rather tired body.

"I am okay."

"Are you upset?" My concern visibly getting on her nerves by now.

"I am fine. Just go away. You don't have time for me anyways." The truth in her sharp words hurt, replacing the feeling of annoyance with that of guilt.

I transitioned to sharing mode and narrated some weekend stories from the MBA program. Then, as Naveli warmed up to my animated stories, I slid my question, "Hey, how is it going at school? Anything new? interesting? or dull?"

Like a stone falling on a delicate glass plane, my question snapped her out of the warmth we had just started building together. She got up from the bed and turned towards me

as she shouted back, "You know nothing about me. Zero. I am not the girl you think I am anymore."

"Connected" was a game I had devised over the years to strengthen the connection with my daughters as they navigated the ups and downs of the growing-up process. We can obviously not set up a structured one-on-one or bring them a questionnaire to gaze their sentiment or engagement at home like we can with our teams at work. Instead, at home I planned activities and indulged in games and conversations to learn about my daughters. Then sometimes, my analytical brain would ask them to score me on "how much I knew about them." They would occasionally blurt out individual answers and, other times, debate where I stood. We called this our "Connected" score.

In their elementary school years, my score remained in the high nineties. Mysterious smiles felt it appropriate to deduct a few points for my lack of awareness of the empty Oreo cookie pack sitting in the pantry after a delicious cookie and milk feast. In middle school, the score dipped to a low 90%. "We are not sharing our friends' secrets with you," Naveli had commented. I took pride in her integrity towards her friends and comfort in sharing such with me. I had expected the score to fall as she entered high school but had never imagined a zero. It was terrible, really, bad. It hurt my ego on all fronts as it made me guilty.

I had hoped to hit the bed soon that night, tired after a grueling work week followed by a finance and strategy filled weekend. But now my brain was fixated on Navi.

When I knocked on the door again, this time with her favorite dish, *harira* (a sweet, medicinal soupy dish made of semolina and turmeric), she let me in. She also figured out a way to maintain her "not talking to you" decision while honoring my persistent pleas for conversation. She picked up her iPod. Played "She's So Gone" from Lemonade Mouth and settled to slurp on the harira in the comfort of that song. We had a conversation for the next hour or so - my words paired with her choice of songs. In front of me stood a courageous teenager willing to challenge the status quo, tears rolling, yet firmly holding her ground to feel heard. I learned about the richness of the pieces in her library, her fears, and her assumptions. And I learned about myself. It was perhaps one of the most meaningful conversations we had had in a long time.

It was late at night. We hugged each other, and she whispered, "Maybe 20%." A ray of light had crawled through the cracks. Though the night was evidently going to be a long one.

I hadn't written in my diary for quite some time. That night I picked it up again. It had become my place to vent and reflect. And so, I did just that. *I had made a promise to myself to build a family where conversations could flow freely and openly. Where we could live unbound to the societal roles and rules, instead evaluate them from a new lens. A lens that allowed us to grow individually and together. When did I lose track of it? Why did I lose track of it? I have to find a way to collect these shattered pieces and put them together, for she is broken, and I, too, stretched.*

My always smiling girl was hardly smiling these days. She would lock herself in her room all day. I was now conscious about spending time with her, but it was clear that we needed more time together.

I wanted to build life-changing companies and products, but none would make me happy without the comfort of knowing that I had nurtured the products I had given birth to. I had been the primary parent all along, and the MBA was a short break, with Gunjan now stepping in to parent. He was doing the carpool runs and taking care of school logistics, but something was missing. The girls felt neither connected to him nor me. They seemed aloof, distant. A few months later, I completed my MBA and decided to go all in to focus on the most valuable assets in my life's portfolio, my daughters. I quit my corporate job.

It took eight months of being "always there" to renew our bonds. My connected score finally went back to 90% and my awareness of the four unique souls living together in our house heightened. Each with our own beliefs, traits, skills, and passions. For each of us to grow individually and collectively, we had to stay open to conflicting views. We had to understand the merits of honest conversations and devise techniques to remain an effective team.

Manisha's Diary

March 2003 - Parenting Product Management

I am decent at my job. I have successfully built technology products and am steadily improving in that trade. I have methodologies to track my progress, mentors to fast-track my growth, and many opportunities to attend professional trainings.

I never had an opportunity to train as a parent, though. Several opinions were offered, often conflicting, but none provided a concrete perspective. Every day, I fear failing to be the parent my daughter needs. As I cross the chasm from work to home, I keep visualizing my deathbed during my drives back home and wondering if I would be happy to be a successful professional or miserable for failing in what had started to become the most crucial aspect of my existence, being a parent.

I have been ambitious. I still am. I have overcome several challenges to evolve into the person I am becoming. I love dreaming big dreams and taking on the challenge to make them real. I am addicted to figuring things out, learning, stumbling, stretching, and sometimes winning. I have failed many times, but something always seems to work out. Maybe because I am built to not give up. Or maybe Mother Luck wants me to succeed. Maybe that is why I am addicted to wanting it all and wanting to ace it all.

We have been married for almost three years, and I have learnt how marriage tends to double our responsibilities and halve our time. Parenthood has further accentuated that mathematics compounds our obligations higher and our time further down. But why this constant guilt. The little girl inside me is still full of dreams and hopes. But the person camouflaging her is buried in new responsibilities. She keeps double-guessing, self-doubting. She is unhappy.

Naveli is just eighteen months old. My poor girl was clinging to me, crying, wanting me to pick her up after spending all day at daycare. I was tired after a day's work and wanted to finish cooking fast. I hoped the swing would soothe her and I could finish cooking. Why was Gunjan late? Why didn't the swing comfort her? Why did I have to cook?

Tonight, she sleeps with me, not in the crib. More to overcome my guilt rather than for her comfort. The clouds of self-doubt are looming heavy around my abilities to be a good parent. I have no idea how I will overcome this. But I know I want to understand her. I want to make her count. And I want to lead by example by making myself count.

Maybe I can start with merging my two worlds - one in which I fare well and another in which I desperately want to excel. Maybe I can connect the parent and the product manager in me to venture into Parenting Product Management to raise a confident child.

Conflict and Compassion

The fine line.

Nitya

Don't expect, ask.

When I was younger, I always wanted to be liked. I wanted to do whatever I could to please others, especially those who seemed to already be appreciated. I saw that everyone would be friends with you if everyone liked you. If you are friends with likable people, you become associated with that likability. So basically, I was a people pleaser. And while there is nothing wrong with wanting to create a good impression, there is a lot wrong with doing that out of compulsion and insecurity, often at your own expense.

The first time I experienced this was in elementary school. This was when rainbow loom bracelets, DIY slime, and cute mini stationery supplies like washi tape were big. And I, who enjoyed arts and crafts, had an extensive collection of colorful sharpies and tape-fittings that I cherished.

One day, a friend of mine asked to borrow my collection. While I resisted at first, I wanted her to like me, so I gave her my entire collection, expecting her to return it soon. Instead, after a few months had passed, she still didn't return it. I wanted to ask for them in the back of my mind, but I feared coming across as mean. When she finally returned, the tapes were almost over, yet I didn't say anything to her. These were items I savored and used prudently. A small cutting of these tapes used well can decorate a card or a gift. The person had indeed used them wastefully. This learning wasn't about the tapes for me but about learning to lend only and only if I felt comfortable doing so.

Technically, my friend in this situation did nothing wrong. However, I was mad because I had created an expectation in my mind, and I expected my friend to somehow understand this without my telling her.

The next time I found myself in a similar situation was in a group project. I had done my share, and I expected my group members to do their part. But when they wouldn't, and the deadline was approaching, I nudged and reminded them. I realized how easy it was to get people to deliver when you can politely but assertively manage people and set clear expectations.

In a more mature context, one of the most pertinent places this applies is group dinners. When you go out in a big group, people often don't split the bill ten ways. One person pays and then the other pays that person back. The issue with taking on this responsibility is that while it seems convenient at the time, taking up this job full-time means you may have to hunt others down in order to get your money back at the cost of feeling odd for asking.

There are two solutions to this. One, you avoid the role all together. Or two, you set expectations straight on getting your money back. If you're the one paying, you can ask people to pay you back in the moment or tell them when to pay you back rather than asking. This way expectations are set in a way that isn't demeaning to anyone. And you don't find yourself feeling uncomfortable when asking for your own money back.

Naveli

The Friendship Bracelet

Through my wild college rides, I recently dealt with issues that we face as we grow up to become mature adults.

Starting at UC Davis in September 2019, right before my eighteenth birthday, college felt like a push in the wild. Suddenly I was unsheltered. I was entirely in charge of my life, time, energy, academics, and health. Everything. Yet it was nothing unique as many were in a similar boat.

I was in a suite in Cuarto's part of campus during my first year. Two rooms connected by a private bathroom housed six people instead of the dorm layouts in most colleges with doubles and triple rooms and communal bathrooms. Luckily, for most of my stay in Cuarto, one of the two rooms remained unoccupied. So, I only had two roommates, and we shared a bathroom.

Typical roommate issues like showering schedules, thermostat regulations, and late-night light/sound nuisances surfaced. There were times when it became difficult to communicate.

I started understanding the importance of managing expectations, not just with my friends but also with my family. I would often take the Amtrak back home over the weekends. It became the route for the fall quarter as my home was close and comfortable. But I realized I couldn't be doing that, not in college. Weekends are when people explore and get to know one another. Weekends were busy with schoolwork. If I was not in Davis during the weekends, I would be coming in my own way to establish a healthy social life, something I did not want to do. So, I changed my routine during the winter quarter, my last in-person quarter of first year and established a new norm with my family.

In sophomore year, I shifted from dorms to an apartment. And yet, I never really lived in that space; the pandemic had a full-blown hit. As a Bay Area student going to UC Davis (an hour and a half away), it didn't make much sense to stay in a pandemic-ridden Davis. In the apartment, my at-the-time good friend was also my housemate.

As things settled, I decided to move into my apartment a few months later. To navigate the pandemic, we needed some baseline rules for our apartment. Unfortunately, my housemate had one idea, and I had another, leading to a stark disagreement. Conflict arose quickly, and we failed to resolve it amicably, leading to a fallout. It doesn't really matter who was right or wrong now. What I learned was that I had failed to manage expectations. As a result, we strained our relationship, and I could not move into my own apartment.

I moved back full-time to Davis in a different apartment with two other housemates during my junior year. Now I stay back over weekends. But, as we all strive to grow and mature, college mates being always there can create their own type of struggles.

Sometimes, being friends with housemates can be tricky because of conflict of expectations across the two relations. Housemates are expected to be always willing to help and be there for you, while we are more understanding of friends not being able to step in at times. I have both experienced and expected this of my housemates. There are times when simply because I know one of my housemates is home, I will go and want to rant to them, with complete disregard for their time. They, too, have returned similar, uninvited favors.

A recent example: one of my housemates gets bothered by dirty dishes in the sink. A tiny sink with only one single bowl, even a small pile of dirty dishes makes it challenging to wash big pots or even small dishes when we cook. I was never good about my dishes for the last maybe seven years. Mumma would get annoyed at my habit of leaving dirty dishes on my table or in the sink. I would reassure her, "I was going to clean them." She would get a bit madder and question, "When will this almost become already," and move on. And though I intended to work on that habit I had developed, it wasn't something I had ever actively committed to resolving.

Over the past two months in Davis, there have been numerous times when I have left my dishes in the sink, anticipating that I would clean them later. All good intentions but no action. I would keep putting it off. Finally, my housemate talked to me about this reoccurrence. I promised to improve, but it happened again. My housemate was offended. She shared that my behavior had impacted her view of our friendship and asked for her space, distancing herself from me. An unintended and harsh consequence for a dirty dish, it felt. So, I became intentional about my dishes to mend our friendship and to follow through on the promises I had made earlier to my mom.

I find it somewhat difficult to raise concerns about things that bother me in the house. I sometimes feel like I will cross the line into being "bitchy" or "rude." On the other hand, my housemates have seemed to define the line well and yet still are compassionate.

The issue of the dishes led me to realize that I had problems of my own that I had suppressed. Mainly because I was uncomfortable to be seen as rude and bitchy to my peers. I love staying in my room, as I can study and do whatever I want in my room (make it as messy as I want). In contrast, one of my housemates likes to work, paint, bead, get ready, and watch TV in the living room; she likes the change of pace rather than being in her room. It is all good except that she leaves the living room a mess, making it a hassle to clean when I have guests. Occasionally, it becomes a deterrent for me to even have people over.

I realized that I had to say something to her about the mess and the issues it has created for me. So I decided to raise my concerns, set expectations, and hoped to resolve any conflicts that may have been brewing in the process.

An hour-long conversation helped us resolve the conflicts and understand each other better. As a result, a new equilibrium was established.

Conflicts arise. It is natural when we live together. We don't need to suppress them as that only results in angst. Instead, with clear and honest communication, we can address these conflicts constructively, which in the long run only strengthens our relations.

———

I had learned this lesson before in elementary school. I was nine years old, in fifth grade, with the exciting prospects of a grown-up middle school and the possibility of everlasting friends. My fifth-grade friends, I thought, were my best friends for my entire life. The cusp of elementary and middle school is the age when everything seems like it's finally clicking together. When our perceived value-based ideologies start becoming the basis of friendships as we transition from physical tributes and possessions to loyalty and intimacy.

I was creative, and I liked making things for my friends. I was obsessed with beading. Making bracelets, necklaces, and jewelry became a form of endearment for me. It was often a gift that I would feel proud to make and give. The focus of my fourth-grade birthday party was, in fact, beads. Twenty of my friends gathered in our family room to make bracelets and necklaces.

In fifth grade, as we prepared to transition to middle school, the idea of creating "best friend jewelry" with my three closest friends popped up. We were all for it. I was excited. As we walked past the tanbark on the playground, one of them had commented, "Every best friend group has store-bought jewelry. We will be unique. We will make them."

Since I was the one who had beads at home, the onus was given to me to make them first. I thought of making four bags with the same exact beads for them to customize yet make somewhat similar bracelets.

Back then, I was always on top of my academics. For the next few days, schoolwork and extracurricular took up most of our time, and beads took a back seat. The excitement of making these bracelets started to fade a little. I started hearing, "Maybe we buy our bracelets," but I maintained my stance. "We will make them. I will get you the beads too."

Then one day, I decided to just go ahead with the plan. I sat in my room for hours, sorting through the beads - dividing the fake pearls, evil eye pendants, red glass stones, and countless ovals into four sets. I did so until I found the perfect blend of whimsical colors that signified our friendship and bond with each other. Those four bags were absolute perfection. All they had to do now was make the bracelets.

As I took those bags out the next day, my friend said, "Oh, Naveli, I have something for you."

Then another one chirped in, "Yeah, we went to the store this weekend and found these adorable necklaces and decided to just buy them as a symbol of our friendship." My heart sank, and I quickly put the bags back into my backpack.

It was a cute necklace and a worthy sentiment. But it wasn't the expectation we had set. All the hard work I had put into creating the perfectly unique friendship bracelets was abruptly shattered.

I don't remember much about the argument that ensued on that playground. Memories fade and sometimes remain jaded when we reflect on childhood events. But I remember them saying that the entire point was simply to get *something* that symbolized our friendship. They had forgotten our pact to invest our efforts into our friendship. So, in their eyes, they made things easier. But for me, the sinking feeling of betrayal and hurt was there. They couldn't comprehend the problem in their decision to change the plan on a whim in a store. All without keeping me in the loop while I had spent the entire evening immersed in the sea of beads preparing our perfect friendship bags. I had wished for friends who could connect, make decisions, and understand each other. Enjoy each other. Talk to each other.

That emotion is prominent still to this day.

We stayed friends halfway through middle school, then drifted apart as we evolved differently. But conflicts and resolutions became a defining construct for relations in my life.

Naveli's Diary

Balancing compassion and conflict have always been a struggle. It's been a critical point in many discussions with my friends and Mom. Yet, I am still learning what that line is and how to define it.

Compassion

*When courage falls short,
compassion makes us stronger.*

Family

Naveli

Shared below are snippets from my memory book assembled to paint a picture of the emotional turbulence as we learn the meaning of a family.

Belong

A room with love. Joy and laughter, yes
But comfort all the same.
The feeling of sinking into
A comfy couch takes over. A safe place.
Laughter, echoes, and smiles fill that room with joy.
Ignorant bliss in the air.
Baritones boasting. Octaves bouncing
Wall-to-wall. A happy place like home.
A different room. A debate. Furrowed eyebrows
Shouting voices with power like thunder.
Ground shaking. Fingers pointing. To tone, with
No end in sight. A powerful place filled with anger.
Water flows down over the crevices.
Face droopy. Water dropping. Sniffles muffled in the air.
Bodies slumped. The air smells of chaotic
Melancholy. A sad place.
At some point in life
There will be moments…
Moments when you feel safe
Moments when you feel home
Moments when you feel angry

Moments when you feel sad
All cyclical moments. Yet many more to come
Moments fleet, yet one lingers–
Its touch burns a hole in your memory.
I am there.
A place that I could call home
But
Not a single place
That I belonged.
This was that moment for me.
-Naveli

My Mom's a Bitch

The importance of family has been challenging to grasp. No, not in the way of understanding that they love me. No, not in caring for them or them caring for me. Not even how we come together to form a familial nuclear unit. But in the way of genuinely valuing each other.

I was a pretty rebellious teenager. A fact. We can accredit that to being the first child, my peers around me, the generational gaps, or societal pressures that instigated my lack of empathy and recognition for my family.

2017 was an exciting time. I was a sophomore, focused on academics, swaying through the ups and downs of high school. At the same time, the constant turmoil and hormonal waves hit me like a thousand bricks. I had finally found a place for myself in the world. I had acting rehearsals for Kronos, Mastane captaincy, CharityDress responsibilities, and the ever-gloomy SAT prep. I was busy, but more importantly, I had found a community that accepted me for who I was.

I used to make many friends. I used to call many of them "my closest" or even "best friends." Then Mom's words were ingrained in my head and my heart. Friends are not "automatically best friends." But, over time, they can become best friends as we win each other's trust. This concept of "friendship levels" initially felt absurd, but it started making sense as years passed by.

The select few I referred to as my best friends now had been with me for good enough time. Layers of closeness had established the intimacy of these friendships. These were to be my friends for the rest of my life. These were to be the people to guide the way and build memories through fun and woes.

A quarter of the way through the academic year, I met someone through a close friend who eventually would change my life trajectory. We developed romantic feelings for each other, and soon he was my boyfriend.

After that first ZAP and its subsequent make-up in middle school, I improved, but I turned lax about deadlines in high school. I got distracted, and my work ethic saw a stark decline. As I digressed from my studies, my parents weren't super supportive of me having a romantic love life to limit the distractions around me. So, I didn't tell anyone at home about him.

He was from a different school. Through him, I met new people, increasing my social depths. My social life boomed, but my ambivert nature sometimes couldn't handle it, constantly losing grip on reality. I was giving in to the animate urge to fit in and looming in the dark clouds of rebellion at home.

Eventually, Mom found out about him between my ongoing academic struggles and frivolous and frequent fights about autonomy, independence, morals, and values.

One day after I returned from teaching a dance class, I locked myself in my bathroom with my phone, texting away angrily. The established deal by that time was no phone in the toilet. I was to surrender my phone to my parents during study time. I was obstreperous; I didn't care. Two minutes later, Mom realized that I had disobeyed. Banging on the door, with an angry raised voice, she told me to come out.

After a few minutes, I finally did.

"Open the phone," she demanded.

"No. Why? I am giving it to you now. Why does it matter?"

"Just open the phone."

Afraid of what could happen and knowing that she was furious at me, I reluctantly put in my password. Click-click-click-click-unlock.

"Give it to me."

I abided.

On the screen. In a blue iMessage box. A text sent by me. 'My mom's a bitch.'

Mom's a bitch- I don't entirely know why I wrote it. I just did. Maybe it was the atmosphere that bred this naivety. Or perhaps the friends I had made and my deep desire to fit in with them. Or the prevailing ABCD (American Born Confused Desi) attitude.

No matter what the reason, there it was. Written. Sent. To my close friends.

Slouched and defeated, Mom turned and walked away. With my phone in her hand, staring at the screen.

But I overlooked that. I was just aware of the red in my eyes. The annoyance grew by the second for not being able to use my phone.

Later that night, I went up to Mom, still angry. "It's my phone. Can I have it back?"

"It's my house. You cannot."

"Why are you trying to govern me? Let me be. I made a mistake. I won't date. Whatever. But stop controlling me. Stop being a . . . Biting back the word 'bitch,' I stopped mid-sentence.

"Bitch?" Her voice wavered. "You don't know anything about having a bitchy mom. I can be one if you like. But I don't want to be like that even if it's cool to call moms names these days."

After a brief pause, she continued, "I understand peer pressure. Confide in your friends, but there isn't really a need to do it at the cost of your family. So often at work, parents talk about their child's rebellion. While I empathize with them, I try not to fit in artificially by talking ill about you."

The pang of hurt hit my stomach. Suddenly, I felt a wave of remorse. But the anger overpowered me. "You never let me be. You always have to control me. To make me do whatever you think is right. I don't care. Just give me my phone back!"

It took almost a year to figure out how incorrect that sentiment was. I went through a break-up, changed schools, fought and won over the fake friends, abandoned social media, changed my phone number and friend circle - my mom stood by my side at every step. She cared in her own way. Even to the extent of not caring about being seen as a bitch by my naive eyes.

As I moved out of our home to pursue college, my understanding of the family connection grew more profound. I started missing my family and, somehow more so, the stability and guidance they provided. I felt privileged to have such a close-knit family. Internalizing the impact of trustworthy relations during my growing years, I found a new love and adoration for my mom, Dad, and sister.

The pandemic's beginning was a mix of emotions in the household. Mom was equanimous; Nitya was ecstatic; I was disheartened; Dad was stoic. Six months of distance of me being out from home had impacted the family. Communication had weakened between all of us in general. Our growing differences of opinions became noticeable as we were forced back into the family unit.

I remember this one explosive argument among all four of us. The sky was dark, the breeze humming by. We were seated on the couch and ottomans in the living room, trying to voice our opinions and be heard. The argument is hazy now, but I vividly remember that I found a new role for myself in the family.

We all have opinions. And we have all become very comfortable in sharing them. Which sometimes makes it difficult to understand one another in heated situations. Somehow that day, I became the mediator. Directing one person to speak while the other stayed quiet, giving the rest a chance to respond. Periodically, I would also restate what I had heard and, if required, use trump cards based on my learning about human psychology.

Then throughout our discussions and arguments, I stepped in to mediate if I felt necessary. An addition to the family's *pitara* (keepsake box) is a new joke, "Naveli's the mediator; it's going to happen."

And though they say it jokingly, I know they appreciate my efforts to bring us together.

Naveli's Diary

It takes time to understand the love of a family. Whether far or near, having a family means we are always loved, and we will always love.

Nitya

The Elephant In the Screen

Didi and I shared a room. Fights were considered a normal part of growing up with a sibling. With time I had discovered a new comfort in understanding Didi's perspective. But I still struggled to understand my role and, more importantly, its limitations within a family setting, explicitly the part of being the youngest.

When we are the youngest in the family, our age seems to play a highly discriminatory role in our life. Of course, they say "age is just a number," but that number decides many things - things you are told and things you are shielded from. I understand that there are many factors' parents consider when deciding on family rules. However, the reality is, that sometimes, these rules make us feel cut off. At least, I felt that way often.

It starts to feel isolating when age, a factor you can't control, decides the exposure we get rather than our actual maturity level. Let us take, for example, provocative scenes in movies. It doesn't require a full-blown sex scene; the kissing scenes were enough to make things awkward during family TV time. Then follows the dreaded moment kids sweat on as we start playing the guessing game of "what happens next?"

Next, we cycle through the choices in our head (a) they will skip making it a win-win for all, (b) they tell me to close my eyes, (c) nobody will say anything, so try to stare at anything but the screen or your parent's eye. Honestly, I've always wondered if it's that awkward for parents as well? Do they also undergo the agony of staring at the invisible elephant sitting inside a fifty-inch TV screen?

My friends' families often opted for answer choice (a). But Mom convinced Dad that we get the exposure within a family setting than be clueless and seek answers elsewhere. So, our family rules, though age governed, were a bit relaxed. Mom and Dad let us watch certain scenes that quenched my personal curiosity and slowly (very, very slowly) squashed the tension across age groups in the room.

Mom and Dad often went out of their way to give us rich experiences. In addition, Mom was quite open to exploring seemingly unacceptable paths within our culture and society. So, we ventured from swimming in the ocean to swimming with the dolphins, skydiving, snorkeling, and random adventures like visiting a mosque in Dubai, dancing right in front of Burj Khalifa in Dubai and the waterfalls in Hawaii, ice skating in the US, camel riding in India ...you get the idea. We also visited homeless shelters, an incarcerated camp, orphanages, a home for lepers, a school for differently-abled - all to widen our understanding of the world. Dad too caught on and took us for gun shooting.

This system of nurturing curiosity made me feel heard, which made it easier for me to understand some of the restrictions. Furthermore, I was assured that they would answer my questions once they thought I was ready.

As I grew up, so did the concept of crushes and dating. Boys; males, XY chromosomes; whatever you want to call them. Mom had tried every rule in the book when it came to them. She started by prying out crushes from me in elementary school. Those days the giant smile on my face was enough to give away answers to all her questions. She never really gave her opinion on dating, but she would attempt to poke around the subject.

Next came middle school when people started asking each other out. The sixth and seventh grades breezed by before I needed to use my poker face. Then, in eighth grade, I was asked out by about a dozen guys, most of whom I viewed as friends. Although I didn't open right away, this new influx of male attention, also perhaps attraction, stressed me out. It began to take a mental toll on me. I thought of seeking advice from my friends but was skeptical of the "drama" such conversations would often create at school. I decided against the gamble, and instead, I went to Mom.

Mom understood just the right amount to comfort me without requiring me to divulge many details. She assured me that I need not rush into anything I didn't want and, more importantly, assured me of her support whatever my decision be. However, while she was supportive of my decision, I noticed her partisanship against school-age dates. And so, when the time came that I met the guy I genuinely liked, I was hesitant to tell Mom. Hesitant... but not closed off.

Then came high school. In my first year, I met someone, and we got close towards the end of the school year. Eight months later, through online calls and whatever limited contact we could afford during the virtual school year, we were dating by the January of sophomore year. His entire family, including his two older sisters, knew. And yet I never quite gathered the nerve to tell Mom. I sensed that she had sensed something was on, but still, I kept mum.

Although we had always been open, and she had even shared her comfort with me dating in high school, I had chosen to not share. My silence was fed continually by - Mom's disapproval of Didi's high school relationship, my lingering fear of being distracted from studies, and a recent streak of anger upon Mom's unusual invalidation of my emotions. Didi had once shared the standard rule of telling parents after a few months of dating, once the relationship was stable. And so I kept stalling, telling myself I would when I was ready, and... when my grades were at an all-time high.

Perhaps, I knew exactly what she would say and that she would be right. My grades weren't exceptional at this point. One of the grades was low despite my best efforts as the class was, without a doubt, challenging. The other was low because I was indeed slacking. While none of these reflected my relationship, I was afraid that "he" would be labeled a "distraction."

Unfortunately, all the secrecy ended in vain. While walking the dogs, Mom caught us sitting on a bench together. She kept walking silently. I thought I had seen her. Later that evening, I walked home, confused and scared. This time she chose to be silent, and I decided to talk to her, still unsure if the person I had seen was indeed her.

She wasn't mad at me for having a relationship but rather for keeping it from the family. I knew I had hurt her and broken her trust. That night I got a text. "I am glad you are growing up. Still there is no space for lies and deception in my world. We could have celebrated together. I learnt today that I am not invited to the party anymore. Take care of yourself."

The next day I went to Mom and explained my hesitation in telling her. She was upset but open to hearing me out. She asked about him and his choices, what I liked about him, and how well we got along. As Mom sat silent and I answered her questions, I had somewhat of an epiphany. Perhaps I was afraid of telling her, sensing that she would point out what I knew to be correct, that we wouldn't work out. I think we had both felt it already but were afraid of accepting the consequences, fearing that we couldn't go back to being friends, the good friends we once were. The stress was, in fact, fostering toxicity more than positivity in our relationship.

A relationship should help both people feel like the best versions of themselves. But, unfortunately, it didn't as I was more focused, and he was more relaxed. I wanted to excel at school, and he wanted me to maximize the time we hung out together. My drive to meet new people clashed with his introverted nature. And while these differences had added to our mutual fondness earlier, our differences seemed beyond fixable after living through them.

A week later, we broke up.

In the journey to understand my emotions, I had chosen to deviate away from family. However, somehow Mom still knew just the right things to say and ask even that day. This time I didn't fail to notice - Mom's initial openness, putting me in my place when I messed up, and then still being there for me.

I am comfortable talking to her about guys, but I have also experienced how every coin has two sides. Sometimes we can make parents feel excluded, ruining the fun of the relationship and creating an awkward, isolating distance between us.

Manisha

Parenting by far has to be the primary job for us humans. But, for that matter, any species must evolve, stay relevant, and become stronger through our offspring.

To understand life's true nature, we must integrate logical, scientific thinking with unexplainable yet astute human intuition. But unfortunately, our twisted world kept pushing me myopically only towards logic. Amusingly the philosophies and doctrines for raising kids contradicted themselves, leaving behind nothing but a few ideas to be tried at my own risk. For example, the judgment on breastfeeding is heavily influenced by the author's cultural background and the timeline for the article, making it possible to win both the affirmative and the negative aspects of the debate. Should humans breastfeed? If so, for weeks, months, or years? Should we supplement? If so, when should we start? Is honey, okay? or is it not okay? ...

Another ongoing debate is about the baby's sleep. Should the baby sleep with the parents or in a crib? Should the crib be in a different room? Psychology departments continuously share studies depicting the long-lasting merits of a human cuddle at infancy and also debate if too much interdependence cripples a child's ability to become independent.

When born, we lean heavily on intuition until adults steer us towards hard-core logic. I think our strength is in balancing both. As I navigated the journey from being a daughter to a wife and then a mom, I tried to learn by reading, listening, and observing the kids. They offered the perfect balance to the logical theories adults believe are valid.

For example, no adult debate on the need for women to lean in at work could win against the zero Naveli had *felt* to be the righteous score for me being gone. I had to empathize with her to help her overcome her loneliness, as logical debates would have only distanced us further. Similarly, to understand Nitya's growing affinity for friends and boys, I had to remind myself of my childhood feelings and allow her space to mature at her pace. They will grow up, and they, too, might appreciate logic as we see it. So, I tried being cautious, not to let my impatience weaken our connection. I tried to just be and let them become.

A Belief
The primary goal of any species is survival and evolution.
If so, our primary job then is
Parenting.
Parenting not to guard her
The difference between her and me
Is but my age and perhaps some experience?
Parenting not to mold her my way,
But to set her free,
For her spirits might be brighter and larger than mine.
Although,
Parenting to create a future brighter than our present,
Plays a role.
Fostering emotional confidence, compassion,
Competence, a compass to navigate the worldly noise,
Plays a role.
Parenting to make her feel loved,
Empowered, yet grounded in reality
Plays a role.
Parenting to enable her
To become her best in the world
Plays a role.
Parenting to encourage her to live consciously,
And become her best for the world
Plays a role.
- Manisha

Intersectionality

The Shape of Us - Our Birth Lottery

Naveli

During my senior high school year, we were offered a seminar course called Radical Love for history credit. *Sounds interesting*, I thought. So, guessing what it might entail, though unknowing the exact content of the course, I enrolled.

I signed up for an offbeat class in high school - radical love. As we went through the syllabus, I heard the words "spectrums," "femininity," "LGBTQ+," and "community" repeatedly. I was intrigued. I found a new definition of a term I had not heard of before, an umbrella term that addressed all my identities - Intersectionality.

Intersectionality has become a definitive core word throughout my studies and life. The idea is that we all have many different identities that work together and form who we are. When I first heard this, I thought I knew my identity. I was a student, a daughter, a dancer, a teacher, a sister, and an Indian. These attributes made me who I was. But in reality, what I really was - was wrong.

Intersectionality was not *just* about our roles - being a sister or daughter, student or teacher. It was about our identity: the thoughts we are born with and the things we cannot control. These together make us who we are and, more importantly, define who we are seen as. Unsurprisingly, my ability and privilege had blinded me from these vital aspects of my identity.

I experimented with my first women's studies class at college, where I truly began grasping the concept's complexity. Intersectionality had a broader perspective. It combines six primary tenets and how *intersectionality* they work together - **Gender. Ability. Race. Class. Nation. Sexuality.**

Intrigued and pursuing further knowledge, I delved deeper into related courses. Finally, in understanding and addressing the historical oppression and generational misgivings that women have experienced, I began finding the answer to my question. *Why do people do the things they do, whether good or bad?*

**

During winter break, I came back home for a few weeks. One morning, while I was studying, my cousin and her friend came for an impromptu visit. Mom and Niti joined us in sitting around the circular wooden dining table, chai cups in hand. As conversation fostered, somewhere, I dropped the word - Intersectionality.

"Yes, I remember. Looking at an intersectional lens is important, especially in this political climate. We were just talking about this with some friends a few nights ago," my cousin chimed in.

"Intersectionality?" Mumma looked curious.

"Do you know what that is?" my cousin asked.

"No. Explain." She turned to me, perhaps because I had been the one to mention it initially.

"Intersectionality is the concept that we all have many identities that work together to make us who we are," I said.

"Oh, so basically, just like our concept of a Swiss knife? All the different strengths we carry within us?" I had heard Mom talk about Swiss knives many times. Just like a Swiss knife can perform many things, she had this concept of developing several skills to broaden your horizon and a secure future. But intersectionality was a different concept. Our Swiss knife is about the strengths we develop that become a part of our identity. Intersectionality is about the six inescapable tenets we are bound to that shape our identity.

"No. Not really." Unsure of how to proceed in helping Mom understand the difference between the concepts, I halted.

Luckily my cousin's friend chimed in, "Think about all the things you are born with. Let's take you, for example. You are a female. That is your **gender**. You are Indian. That is your **race**. You are straight. That is your **sexuality**. You are middle class. That is your **class** in society. You are from India but live in the United States. That is your **nationality**. You have a functioning body in that you are what is defined as able-bodied. That is your **ability**."

"All of these aspects of yourself are not learned. Rather, aspects that grant different privileges in life," I added.

"Why is understanding all of this important? Why must we look at them all together as intersectionality rather than separate as six tenets that make us who we are?" Nitya questioned.

"This may help," my cousin tried helping again. "Let's look at a hypothetical person, someone who gets the shortest end of the stick in our society today."

"We can call her Fatima," I added.

"Let's say, Fatima, our character, is a lower-class lesbian, of Middle Eastern origin, living in the US. She has the 'worst' combination of all the traits in terms of societal privileges." my cousin's friend tried making things concrete with an example, which I carried forward. "Basically, she lost tremendously in the birth lottery - starting with the gender lottery. In terms of the race lottery, though, being of black origin is historically oppressive, with the pandemic, the refugee crisis, and terrorism prospects, being of Middle Eastern origin is equally if not more damaging in a societal view. Being from a lower class, she is likely already deprived of resources you and I may take for granted."

Mom and Niti were listening intently.

My cousin clarified things further. "Now compare the opportunities Fatima might have with ours. She will probably get fewer opportunities simply because of her birth situation. As a result, fewer doors will tend to open for her. So, we try to understand others by understanding their intersectionality and accepting that people born on different points on the birth lottery spectrum tend to be luckier than others."

I was silent, observing.

Mom seemed to understand. "Got it. It is not the same as a Swiss knife. Your explanation is in tune with our reasons for visiting the orphanages and working with Dharavi, the biggest slum in southeast Asia. To get perspective beyond our own lives."

Later that day, Mom remarked how good it felt to learn from kids and how happy she was to see the table flip, enabling her to learn something different. While Mom's generation didn't grow up discussing such concepts, her lack of exposure was evident, as was her genuine curiosity to learn.

I could perhaps add another aspect to this discussion - the family environment where we take birth. Our home is open for us to attempt to discuss concepts that may still be taboo in many parts of the world — perhaps a privilege for some. It helps. The more we understand the world around us, the more the world seems to understand us.

Naveli's Diary

Looking back, I haven't heard of Intersectionality, just in the women's studies course. Yet, perhaps it was the most abundant in its teaching because a primary societal viewpoint on Intersectionality exists on a core tenet: gender. I can't help but believe that there is a necessity for everyone to understand Intersectionality and all aspects of it. Maybe that was my subconscious goal that day - to make my family understand it, especially Mom.

Spectrums -the gravity of that word and its importance aren't often noted. It's almost as if the more ability and privilege we have, the less we understand it. Or so it seems. Intersectionality, too, lies on a spectrum. One that stretches on six different sides, creating endless combinations. Like our character Fatima who fell on one end of the birth lottery spectrum, we all live on our point combinations. Judging anyone without knowing how birth has treated them only cripples our thinking.

While I grew up in America, Mom and Dad lived in India until their mid-twenties. Both have shared the challenges they faced in accessing quality education and exposure. Mom's learning is to strive by investing in a repertoire of knowledge and experiences - a notion she calls the Swiss knife.

I've had conversations with her before where we observe and occasionally analyze other people's behaviors. Some were insightful - for example, when she noted how effortlessly shopkeepers and baristas handle demanding customers, gracefully without feeling less empowered in their profession. Then there were some of her comments that would make me question her judgment. The occasional: "She has potential. If she worked a little harder, she could scale heights."

Mom was not wrong in her saying. But without recognizing that stranger's Intersectionality, Mom had passed a judgment on others based on her ability in life. Society doesn't make it easy for everyone to fight through. I wanted her to understand this.

Her naive statements would ring in my head - making me wonder if it was so easy for people to make quick judgments; how did others understand me from afar? Or Mom? Or Nitya? Dad? My friends?

It may be selfish that I was looking at it from my perspective. But there was a time when I did want people to pity me and my circumstances. There was a time when I confessed that to Mom. My circumstances, in part, arose because I am a woman.

—

These concepts stick with me because when we look at a person in a working world, we often forget that they have more going on than their job. That there is more to someone than what our eyes see.

Learning about these tenets gave me a purpose in life. When deciding to minor in Women's Studies, I felt a deep need to acknowledge the gaps, work to lower them, and equalize the playing field. Research and classroom discourses directed me to an intersectional feminist lens. Yet, even beyond classrooms, my experiences precluded me from forgetting about such woes.

After studying the effects of capitalism on global care chains, I gained perspective on many other aspects of our society - and how different elements of Intersectionality play a role in governing human lives. Understanding intersectionality helps me and my attempts to battle my climb—that uphill part of the slide that we must first work through to enjoy the journey ahead. I am convinced that a pervasive understanding of intersectionality will help us understand each other and make our collective climbs easier.

Intersectionality and Mom's concepts of Swiss knife go hand-in-hand - understand the gifts we are born with and make choices to make the most out of them. For ourselves, and for others, at least the ones we love.

Compass

*Finding our way through opportunity
and adversity.*

Perspectives

Becoming Ourselves

Nitya

Becoming Me

This book isn't about "How to Be the Perfect Family 101" because this family - my family - is far from perfect. But what we do have is a sense of trust and connection built over a series of open, honest, and sometimes difficult conversations. I hope to have shared this journey with you through this book.

My definition of a family is a unit that sticks together but, more importantly, brings out the best in each other. And one of the most important things my family has taught me about living in the presence of others is being self-aware. How can I expect my family to understand me if I don't understand myself? How can I expect them to help me be happy and thrive unless I invest in seeking that awareness myself?

High school is expected to be a step in that direction as we plan our journeys ahead. But unfortunately, this is not an easy task for most high schoolers, me included. As I tried different pursuits from dance, singing, and visual arts to business, biology, and debate, my mom pushed me to discover my strengths and passions. As a result, I have learned that I can excel in almost everything I attempt. But my curiosity and tendency to spread myself thin sometimes come in the way of living up to my caliber. By being aware of this trait, I prioritized and dropped a few things in favor of going deeper in subjects I wanted to pursue more passionately.

I also learned the concept of reputation. There is beauty in understanding our reputation and that it can work for and against us. I also experienced that many people are tempted to find faults in others in high school. They are creative too. For example, I come across as sweet and peppy to most people. So, I was seen by some as trying too hard and a pushover. While applying for the officer role for the debate club, one of the largest clubs in my school, the head coach teacher expressed this exact concern. She said that while my approachable nature was to my advantage, she worried that the consequence was that I was seen as non-assertive. This awareness about my reputation helped me change perceptions and draw attention to my not visible skills. As a result, I was elected as the club's treasurer based on my ability to be empathetic yet assertive, required to raise and manage the thirty thousand dollars the club needs.

The hardest thing I grew awareness of was my wins and losses. I didn't want to be a person who dwelled in regrets about not trying. Mom always taught us to try new things and open new doors for ourselves. "It's easier to say no respectfully later than to get in once the door is closed."

So, I attempted everything I could.

I won't sugarcoat and call them learning. But, quite honestly, in those moments, after losing elections, not getting an opportunity after a time-consuming application and a grueling interview and getting a bad grade in a challenging class definitely didn't feel like learning.

Yet, it is also true that along with these losses came winning. I won elections, earned internships, was offered paid jobs, and learned to work towards success. I learned to try for opportunities and accept wins and losses as reasonable outcomes. I learned to appreciate life as it comes and to believe that everything happens for a reason. As one door closed, another opened. I just had to keep trying. Harder. Smarter. I grew tougher. I realized how important it was to learn how to rebound back. And I became comfortable with taking calculated risks and handling losses and uncomfortable with playing it safe.

There are so many aspects to a person; it's unrealistic to know them all by high school. But by learning to be aware of my strengths, passions, personality traits, and reputation, I grew to understand myself and my opportunities better.

As I enroll in new classes, I apply this learning to evolve my self-image. It helps me to have a goal, stay open, and adapt as I learn more about myself. For example, everyone thought I would be a lawyer as I was a good debater and researcher. But last year, I grew to love AP Biology and discovered my appreciation for medical sciences. Then this year, I rediscovered how amusing books can be in the AP Literature class. So, after the thousand excuses I cooked up to put my "reading habits" on the back burner since elementary school, I have hooked on books again.

There is no rulebook to life, no rulebook on how to be the perfect person, daughter, sister, girlfriend, or friend. While I am still figuring out what I want to do in my life, I am also learning to understand myself. And this understanding helps me adjust and adapt my choices to become who I want to be.

Naveli's Diary

Unspoken

> *Never do these things happen during youth*
> *Yet, I am lost, unknowing they happen*
> *Now, who would think to ask me the truth?*
> *Black ink flows like snake's venom from the pen.*
> *A hundred pains are spread on the body*
> *Clothes of all compassion are now dirtied*
> *They are left stunned, feeling like nobody*
> *Its harsh whips lash at me; I'm shocked; I'm tied*
> *Though you try to cut the winds with your wings,*
> *You'll never prevent yourself from yourself*
> *You may break the skies and burn all the worlds*
> *Tries bring defeat. Just your soul and yourself*
> *For you may be homeless, sad, and broken*
> *You are a nightingale, left unspoken.*
> *~Naveli*

Naveli

Perspectives

Point of view. POV. Viewpoint. Three terms with the exact same meaning. We've heard of them being used in core and literature classes together with books and titles throughout childhood. First person. Second person. Third person. More examples of views just tweaked to expose altering thoughts.

In sixth grade, I read the book *Wonder* for the first time. With six different narrators exposing me to a whirlwind of contrasting views, I was thrown into figuring out the motivations and purposes of everyone. Perhaps the most obvious example of a formational POV book during my childhood, I latched onto the idea of contrasting views, an intriguing setup, which made the story even better.

Point of view. POV. Viewpoint. Then a fourth was added. An overarching one, not only connotated with analytical experiences. But also, with life experiences. *Perspectives.*

After the unwarranted experiences in junior year, I felt quite alone. No voice. No identity. Somewhere, I wanted to pity myself. Truth be told, I wanted others to pity me too. It seemed only fair, the antidote to the unfair assault, cyberbullying, and the sudden loss of support and friends.

Back then, the world was crumbling around me. And as Mom used the word victim even to help me understand, and as my friends left me to be, I became antisocial. I had justified myself in wanting pity and had begun believing my life was terrible. Lost in my little well, I forgot that others still lived a much harder life. And as my perspective on the world narrowed, I lost my grip on my own world. This was February of 2018.

That spring break, Mom planned a trip to India. It wasn't just a trip to visit family. But ingrained was a plan to seek new projects for CharityDress, the 501©3 non-profit we had started in 2013 to provide clothing and educational opportunities to low-income areas. With India being the most accessible market to us and the demand for technical skills growing there, it was a viable step for CharityDress. We had plans to visit orphanages, ashrams, schools for differently abled and low-income areas, and Dharavi, the largest slum in Southeast Asia.

Mom and I were in long conversations and countless arguments those days. She tried springing me outside my spiral, but I was stuck. Finally, one day, I confessed, "Fine. I pity myself. I want others to understand my pain. This is not #MeToo, Mom. And why did the assault have to happen to me?" I couldn't understand why I was going through such a tough time while my peers seemed to have rose-colored glasses on as they experienced the world. I was sixteen, but the world's gravity weighed down on me.

"You can't take back what happened. You can only move forward. What happened to you was not right. Take time to recover, but you can't wallow. You can't let it define you or suck up your entire life." She took a minute. "You need perspective. What happened shouldn't have. But life has to go on. Don't end it prematurely. Tomorrow has a bright future waiting for you patiently, but not forever. And while it might feel that way right now, if you believe it and repeat the bad happenings in your head, you will repeatedly relive the pain again and again and again. And it is only going to hurt more. I know... I know you are wiser and stronger than that."

I sighed, "Maybe." But the pain was everlasting. It didn't feel there was any way out of it.

"Use this trip as perspective." I didn't know what that meant. Unwilling to talk anymore, I left the conversation.

Two weeks later, we arrived in Bangalore. After spending a day with Nani, Nanu, Mami, Mama, Samarth, and Amay, we visited Jeevodaya Ashram. The pavement was dusty. Behind a cluster of three-story homes and offices. In a tiny crevice of the city that no one might think of looking into. A little one-story building, this was home for about fifteen previously incarcerated women who had been banished from their individual communities. A shelter.

They knew that we would be coming. And perhaps that's why there was formality in the air. One lady was sitting at an old wooden dining table as we walked in. Metal dishes everywhere. She introduced herself and told us to take a seat. As the ladies walked in one by one, I noticed a tiny human clutching one of them. I later found out that this woman had a child in prison; neither the mom nor the child was now accepted by society. Gradually, the wave of tension dissipated into a strength in unity as we talked to them. They had formed their own community, lessening the effect of the abandonment they had each faced in life.

Four hours later, I walked out, back on that dusty pavement, with a feeling of contentment.

The next day, we went to Samarthanam, a Trust for the Disabled. A school, orphanage, and workplace, Samarthanam served the blind of the community around them. This was a place where these children could access books; in association with the Indian government, Samarthanam has its own private collection of recorded audiobooks and stories. We sat in on a class, helping blind kids on their journey with braille and math.

In the middle of the building was an open field with people. I walked closer to find not people but kids on it. I went closer still. The kids were playing cricket. I was stunned as I realized that these were blind kids. They had figured out their ways and rules to play cricket because they wanted to. And because they could. That changed me. As I watched, a kid hit the ball, and the ball bounced off the boundary to create an atmosphere of triumphant hope. I was inspired. And an everlasting hope arose within me. It made me contemplate how I would be living life if I couldn't see. I grew up hearing about Helen Keller, but seeing this offered a reality check on my privilege. The privilege of a fully functional body. The privilege of sight. The privilege of my abilities.

Later that day, we met Abhishek Bhaiya, the CSR (corporate social responsibility) head at Brillio, to explore a connection between their programs and CharityDress's services. My world expanded as he explained the UN's sustainable development goals and delved into his initiatives to address poverty and education issues in India.

The next day we flew to Mumbai to meet a company that built STEM projects, where we picked up a few kits to make solar cars. A few hours later, we were at the Dharavi Diaries, in the heart of the slum. Already in an established relationship with Nawneet Ranjan (founder of Dharavi Diaries), we co-led a workshop to expose local kids to the growing possibilities in technology. Some kids were extremely excited. Coin magnets attracted younger kids. The possibilities of VR and AR became the steadfast goals of others. Some were fascinated with the solar panels, while a few simply decided to stay in the corner and not involve themselves.

That night, as we were traveling back to the airport, Mumma, Nitya, and I discussed the workshop. "Some people take advantage of the opportunities around them. Others don't," Nitya noted.

Mumma responded. "True. I actually went up and tried to involve them."

"I noticed," I noted. "It didn't seem fruitful."

"It wasn't. When I asked the kids to join the workshop, they said they wouldn't be good in this field anyway. Besides, they didn't need to make extra efforts now that the government had subsidized their education."

It is a shame that brief exposure to privilege blinded them from their potential. But, for whatever it's worth, that was a learning for us at CharityDress. A living reminder - that though we may be able to help the unfortunate, unfortunately, we couldn't manufacture motivation for them.

That night, on the flight back to Bangalore, I felt an expanded sense of understanding of my abilities to help and do. I had the privilege of exposure and experiences. Through those trips, under the veil of seeking social projects for CharityDress, I found a sense of self-identity utterly separate from the one I had believed in.

Mom was right. I did get perspective. It's easy to get lost in our thoughts, surrounded by people who sometimes live in their self-built cocoon of thoughts. However, meeting diverse people through these trips brought a new light to life.

Back in America, in the Bay Area, in San Ramon, I pity myself less. Endo grapples with the reality that past experiences don't just go away with new perspectives, but healing becomes much easier.

Recently, I found myself sharing this journey of perspectives and internalizing my privilege with Aachu, my friend-turned-brother. And as I explained these experiences, I gained a broader perspective still.

That was before the lockdown. I have discussed and debated so many more topics with my family in the last few months. And whether in conflicts or conversations, families open the doors to perspectives we seek and need - perspectives that make us aware of our privilege and potential.

Manisha

A Million Indra Nooyis

The alarm made us aware of our nightlong chit-chat catching up from where we had left a few years back. I was trying hard to read the title on the Forbes cover featuring Indra Nooyi when Maansi asked, "What do you really aspire to achieve?"

"Nurture a million Indra Nooyis," I responded and proceeded towards the bathroom.

"Then become one," she smiled, folding the blankets.

That evening, as we leisurely walked through the aisles of the twinkling Dubai malls, she continued, "Why Indra?"

Utterly unprepared for the question, I gazed at our kids walking just a few feet ahead of us. Then reflected, "The freedom that matters most is the freedom to be ourselves. We are born with that sense, though retaining it is hard in a world of societal pressures, sparkling temptations, infinite choices, and non-stop content. Indra Nooyi represents this to me."

"Okay," she nodded.

"Self-awareness has become a virtue. And, even if we become aware, we let ourselves chisel away to fear, societal pressures, confusion, and ambitions." I paused.

"So?" she glanced, then signaled the kids towards the Papparoti store.

I collected my thoughts. "We thrive when we are ourselves, maybe only if we are ourselves. Indra seems to have that, in her personality. And in her upbringing by her forward-looking family, her marriage with a husband willing to follow her lead, her boss willing to give her a chance. It seems like the world kept opening doors for her and she kept walking with her head held high."

We settled at Papparoti and spent a wonderful evening chit-chatting with kids and frivolous, entertaining frolic.

The bonds we create with childhood friends run deep. These bonds lean on a solid foundation of equality. We are just students wanting to learn and have fun. No titles, no bank balance, no castes, gender - nothing divides. It had been hours since we were back home, yet our conversations had continued. Not wanting to sleep still, we decided to make late-night coffee just like we used to in our childhood days. Only then it was to stay up for exam prep. Today it was just to catch up.

She stirred the coffee and sugar concoction as I took the milk out of the fridge.

"What will it take to get there?" she probed.

"Clarity and conviction," I reflected.

"You are good at that."

She left me speechless as I felt the storm she had stirred within.

Nothing, not even a cup of delicious hot coffee, warms the soul like meeting an old friend.

Manisha's Diary

Very Happy

We are born with intellect. Then like sponges, we acquire wisdom or folly from our experiences and environment. My early childhood moments metamorphosed at paradoxical crossroads. I was the inferior girl in the confinement of our boy-favoring joint family, yet superior in socio-economic strata over maids and neighbors. Grandma measured my worth in physical appearance and household chore proficiency. Yet, my equity-seeking parents stayed committed to brightening my future through education.

Then discourses with my freedom fighter grandpa led to debates on freedom. India was independent now. If India was free, why were we still enslaved? Not allowed to be ourselves? Why did we squash curiosity under the labels of insubordination and arrogance, and why did lopsided rituals still replace reason? Why was a fear of the unknown deciding the careers of creative brains and hungry souls? The more knowledge I gathered, the more ignorant I felt.

As the contrasting realities continued to emerge, they became fascinating indulgences. I observed and debated the pros and cons of every situation with a partner if I could recruit one or with myself in the absence of one. The gifts I was born with, paired with my choices, shaped me into a Swiss knife capable of doing many things; yet the lack of clarity on what I really wanted to do kept me restless.

In Vedic scriptures, it is said that the soul takes birth as a human to serve a purpose. Some cultures describe this as the quest to "seek oneself." But how do we decipher our soul's purpose? Ultimately, we all seek happiness, perhaps in our own ways. What does that happiness look like? We seek freedom. The freedom to be ourselves. But what does freedom look like?

Indian weddings give us many reasons to look forward to them. A celebratory atmosphere with colorful dresses, luscious food, friends, music, and dancing. I used to love them until I received the first marriage card from my friend circle. An academically brilliant girl who had barely started college was asked to quit everything and move to a new town to live with a family she had hardly met. The unsettling feeling jolted me to find my path before the world decided my fate.

Build a career, a voice said within. Oscillating between these questions and decisions, I met Gunjan, my now-husband. The construct of marriage brought pressures and biases that have taken shape in years of human evolution. For a period, friends became man and wife, with gender deciding our roles. It helped that Gunjan and I were "friends" and soon consented to let that relation remain the most sacred of all ties between us.

With the birth of my daughters, I was reborn yet again. This time with a higher purpose. From clarity and success for myself to one for them. Now marinating in confusion simmering with marriage, motherhood, profession, and ambition, I looked for ways to help them build their identities without losing my own.

And so began the singular quest to seek awareness, an awareness to be inherently happy. Rumi was astute in his observations - "What you seek is seeking you." Indeed, books emerged, videos surfaced, and frameworks appeared from ancient India and China to coaching from industry leaders and teachers. The jambalaya was rich. I crafted a self-awareness framework to operationalize my learnings.

*To be **V**ery* **HAPPY**, *we need to become aware of our -*

Values *- that lead us through opportunities and adversity*

Happiness *drivers - passions, things we love doing.*

Anchors *- purpose and goals*

Personalities *(traits, biases, behaviors)*

Professional Expertise *- valuable skills and competencies required to earn a living*

Yarns *that weave our life - our responsibilities - parenting, elderly care, etc.*

The first draft for my V. HAPPY puzzle took a few months. It is now a living document updated regularly and checked every summer and winter.

Helping Naveli and Nitya build theirs was a labor of love. Management training is sprinkled with the power of coaching over telling. Yet often, I fell prey to the ease of telling kids what to do. The autopilot kicks in as a tired body and a packed calendar take over the rational brain. But setting an intention made it easier to lean on reflections and open-ended discussions. They built their versions. The value of this framework became evident when they invited me to share it with their friends and teachers. The V Happy framework is happy to have helped more than five hundred people via formal and informal workshops in friend circles, universities, and corporations.

Without clarity, we tend to feel lost, lead a mechanical life, or maybe spend a lifetime victimizing ourselves, unaware of the power we hold within. Awareness offers a feeling of control and the enthusiasm to open doors as opportunities knock. Luck favors. We excel in our right. A happy heart with a competent head builds meaningful connections. We feel worthy. Happiness prevails.

As a wife, then a parent, I felt right to focus on my family. However, the era is changing with Naveli moving towards a job and Nitya toward college. As they prepare to fly out of home into a kingdom of their own, I look forward to life 2.0. Bring this awareness to a billion people with a scalable solution that connects the dots between people and profits.

Humanity thrives when families nurture happy people and work lets them be. Life 1.0 was about family. Life 2.0 will be about work and society.

Epilogue: A Circle Of Trust

Each of us lands in a family and an environment as we arrive in this world. With each day spent together, we shape each other through our lens. Family conversations help us stay grounded and feel comfortable talking and sharing. Our circle of trust starts with our family unit and has branched out to friends and extended family members. Yours may look different and include family, friends, neighbors, cousins, and others who make you feel at home with them.

Families and Circles of Trust do not need official rule books to earn each other's respect. All they need is a genuine effort on our part to become self-aware and aware of others—the effort to want to grow and help others succeed. The attempt to be happy and help others be happy. The effort to talk freely and listen intently. A genuine conviction to make an effort and a commitment to reciprocate others' actions.

In our immediate family unit - NaNiGuMa - openness to conversing with each other has enabled us to learn from one another and has offered new perspectives on sometimes tough or even simple choices.

NaNiGuMa has had ups and downs, but we *want* to converse, and with that mindset, we have been able to. This book only highlights a few things that we've been openly able to talk about, but we've also been on the flip side of it all. There have been times we weren't and still aren't able to freely express ourselves, and that's okay. The empowering feeling is the change in mindset - one wanting to converse, realizing the power we have to help each other with our unique perspectives.

Wanting to converse may also be a Climb. Through the emotional and logistical difficulties, we too, had to condition our mindsets not to hinder the process of trying. Practice helped. The more we felt comfortable conversing, the more we strived to have these conversations. And the less we feel isolated and lonely even when alone, knowing we are just a conversation away from people ready to listen without fear of judgment.

In sharing our family's attempt at connecting and conversing, we hope these stories will break down the typical family and social norms to create an even playing field for people to understand and strengthen each other. And when conversing, we won't have superficial surface level "how are you" and "I'm good" conversations. Instead, have proper conversations. So when we're talking, we are really talking :)

We now turn to you. How will you empower yourself and others in your own Circle Of Trust? How will you make sure that when you are talking, you are really talking? Intently listening and favoring perspectives over judgment?

Appendix: Let the conversations flow

We have stories within each of us, as is our desire to belong and connect. Stories, when shared, spun new ones. So as we shared some of our eye-opening conversations where we learned from each other, our extended Circle of Trust shared theirs. We include some here, hoping they might help your conversations flow.

Trashcan - Tarana Bindal, Age Nine

At school, everyone is fake happy. I was too. But at home, I would express my negative emotions too. When they started feeling that I was negative, I stopped sharing. I sometimes want my family to be my trash can and listen so I can share and get rid of the negativity. Just don't start preaching and teaching all the time.

Slippers - Samarth Gupta, Age Fourteen

I don't particularly appreciate wearing slippers. I neither see this as a problem nor understand why adults waste so much time on frivolous reminders. How can slippers affect my eventual life success? Please let go of small stuff and let me focus on bigger ones. No one walks barefoot once they reach college. Neither will I.

Questions - Amay Gupta, Age Six

It's not fair to question every time I want to do anything - every time I eat candy or want to play. So, every time you want me to study, I will also question.

Incentive - Nitya Garg, Age Twelve

In your mind, when we try to change, others may not see as we make minor improvements. But if we get pushed too hard, the incentive to change fizzles as we start questioning the point of trying when no one appreciates.

Repeating Repetitions - Naveli Garg, Age Fourteen

When you say something too often, the person on the receiving end might not benefit as you expect them to. Sometimes it helps them understand, but ego, emotions, or resistance will often take over and make them irritable. For example, reminders for my teeth problem help me fix them. But reminders of the room messed up when I am watching TV don't - I start dilly-dallying, expecting the repeating reminders to clean up.

As Heard during a Trip to Legoland - Chirag with his daughters, Tarana, Age Eight and Palakh, Age Five

P: What's the plan for tomorrow?

T: Just enjoy the present, Palakh.

P: What's the present?

T: Present is now.

Empowering Begins at Home - Monika with her son Samarth, Age Twelve

A family decision to control Samarth's screen without his consent didn't go well with him. To make his point, he brought up the superficiality of equality and empowerment topics in offices and larger forums without practicing it in our day-to-day lives. It left us thinking about the merit of his argument and the need for children to be involved in family decisions.

Honest Compliments - Rikti Bindal with her daughter, Tarana, Age Eleven

Tarana is a conversationalist, often seen giving compliments to strangers. When questioned, her response was - don't hold back on giving an honest compliment to someone when you get a chance. You don't know what's going on in their day and you can bring a smile/make their day better at least a little bit!

Create Memories - Anita Sanghi with her daughter Aayushi, Age Fifteen

Aayushi told me I should spend my money creating memories because she would earn a lot herself. She kept reiterating her points and even dissuaded me from investing in property in favor of lifestyle.

Finally, I saw the value and started our spree of luxurious holidays, strengthening our bond and making us happier. Maybe kids help with the un-conditioning.

No Yelling - Sherry Shah with her daughter, Myra, Age Eight

Myra's perception of life was a fairy tale, believing that the prince and princess didn't fight. She was surprised at how people talked loudly and yelled at each other. She made us realize that loud voices are noises and take the matter away from the cause and solutions. We get stuck in the ego world and compete on who can yell louder.

Mom Empowerment - Ekta Sahay with her son, Akshat, Age Nineteen

In our family tradition, mothers fast for the long and healthy life of their sons. When Akshat realized that he asked to do it with me for my long life, stating that he would want his mom in the long life. He had only seen mothers and wives pray for the family's well-being. So, his ask was an eye-opener as I should have been the one opening his eyes toward the hardships women go through.

All I Want Is Your Time - Leena Khera with her daughter, Amber, Age Ten

Amber was lonely after Khushi left for higher studies. I used to keep her happy by buying stuff on Amazon. One evening she hugged me when I was on office calls, unable to reciprocate. Later she confronted me. "Can you please stop bribing me with gifts? Give me your time. I am alone in this home." So now I make sure to spend time with her every evening.

Be on Time - Maansi Garg with her sons, Kartik, Age Fourteen and Vinayak, Age Eleven

Kartik and Vinayak are vocal about our habit of coming late to parties. So after being asked a few times, "Why are we always late?" we have made a conscious effort to arrive on time. Their observations and questions shape us to become better individuals.

Expectations - Leena Khera with her daughter, Khushi, Age Fifteen

Khushi is a bright child and fairs well academically. When she was in grade ten, I told her that I had scored one hundred percent in math and expected her to do the same. When I learned how my expectations created anxiety and made it difficult for her to concentrate on the exam, I stopped pressuring my kids on academic excellence. She excelled on her own in eleventh and twelfth grades.

Understand People - Dr. Hari Mohan Gobburu with his daughter, Aasavari, Age Nineteen

I tend to form opinions about people quickly. Aasavari told me that the best way to remove apprehensions and prejudices about people is to spend time with them and understand them. It was an eye-opener, and it works.

Observe Fearlessly - Poonam Rana with her son, Tejjas, Age Seventeen

Tejjas, when two years old, stunned me with his observations like - only our lower jaw moves, and when birds walk with their heads bobbing forward and backward. He helped me learn to keep my eyes and mind open, live in the moment, absorb everything, and learn fearlessly.

Honest Human Being - Sherry Shah with her son, Armaan, Age Sixteen

After an academic conversation, Armaan shared his disappointment in how the system influenced him to think only about his college chances. Then he stated that he would work on being a more honest human being and look after his health.

Resilience - Chirag Bindal with his daughter, Palakh, Age Five

Palakh bounces back quickly from sad/hurtful moments and returns to the present, flipping from sad/crying to a smiling and chirpy kid within seconds.

Doing What's Right - Ritu Agarwal with her daughter, Aarushi, Age Seventeen

Aarushi shared that her close friend was having issues at school and felt we should talk to her friend's parents. Since the topic could be sensitive, we dilly-dallied. A week later, when we still hadn't reached out to them, she reminded us to do what was right without worrying about the consequences of broaching sensitive topics - "If there was something troubling me, wouldn't you as parents want to know?"

Stand Up for Yourself - Neha Rastogi with her daughter, Nysa, Age Eight

When I shared with Nysa that even after a long productive day people can be critical of the progress made, Nysa encouraged me to stand up for myself. Intrigued by her lack of fear, when I leaned in to understand, she said, "It's hard to ignore consequences. Still, my experience is if I don't do that for herself, who else would when Mom isn't around."

Curiosity - Sameer Anand with his son, Kush, Age Twelve

While watching the Nature channel, Kush saw how the earth looked from other planets and asked, "If the earth is round, why don't people fall off it?" Children are born curious, learning about the world through every experience and social interaction.

Lesson from a Bird - Anuradha Govil with her son, Arnav, Age Two and a Half

While watching a bird flying in and out of her nest, Arnav and I discussed how she was fetching worms to keep her babies fed. He responded, "So even in the animal world, the moms go out and work to fetch food for their children. Why don't you go?" I learned that working is okay, and that even the youngest can handle separation from the mommy.

Why Are We Different - Manjusha Deswal with her daughter, Nandini, Age Six

Nandini asked tricky questions – "What is God? What is religion? Who are slaves? Why are boys troubling girls?" She made me think about how equal and straightforward our world starts until we introduce the complexities of constantly differentiating and categorizing.

My Highlight Is You - Ayesha Mathews Wadhwa with her son, Azai, Age Five

Every night we discuss a highlight/lowlight from the day - my husband and I shared work-related things. Then my five-year-old said, "My highlight is right now - with you both." It was a beautiful reminder and a lesson on being present and where we place value.

Daughters Become Friends - Vandana Deep with her daughters, Arshia, Age Twenty, and Ankita, Age Sixteen

During Rohit's hospital stay, Arshia transformed into my friend/ mother/ sister like a role reversal, which gave me a moment of pause. Ankita brings a lot of things into perspective from her lens on how I view and value relationships. I learned the meaning of "being there" from them.

Can't Please Everyone - Anuradha Govil with her daughter, Rhea, Age Sixteen

Rhea once told me that just because everybody says my food is tasty doesn't mean it actually is. I learned not to try to please everyone all the time or to take people's opinions as the ultimate truth.

Things To Think About - Rohit Deep with his daughters, Arshia, Age Twenty, and Ankita, Age Sixteen

We often discuss topics like Black Lives Matter and social equality. Their thought-provoking comments like, "If rich countries or people don't help others in need, who will?" have changed my perspective.

Good at Different Things - Raghavendra Raghunath with his daughter, Eshanya, Age Eight

When my daughter's friend's artwork was getting accolades in the WhatsApp group, I casually asked Eshanya how she felt. I was proud of her reply, "If you think I will be jealous - no. Each of us is good at different things." What we often learn through spiritual practice was inherent in her and came as a refresher course for me.

Things to Remember - Shamshudin Kherani with son, Zaafir, Age Ten, and daughter, Faaria, Age Nine

When Zaafir and Faaria told us that David had won the speech competition at school, I shared that I remembered David. And that he was a respectful boy from the only African American family at school. Farzana, my wife, and I were dumbfounded and felt guilty to hear their disappointment - that the first thing we remembered was David's skin color.

Birthday Cake - Krithika Raghavan with daughter, Nandita, Age Five

"Will I ever be able to eat my birthday cake?" was Nandita's question on her sixth birthday, as her food allergies had restricted her from all eight food allergens. She woke up my creative side in coming up with meals she would look forward to but with limited ingredients. She learned to accept the reality of life and make the most out of what was possible. As a result, Nandita advanced through regular school, unlike most kids with severe allergies who choose to homeschool or seek a 504 exemption.

Eating Right - Raghavendra Raghunath with his son, Chirag, Age Nine

I went to a restaurant to grab dinner before boarding an overnight train. While all of us were choosing dishes we relished, Chirag, who loves eating out, asked for curd rice. "I prefer a light dinner during travel to avoid problems and enjoy the trip." I still try to follow the principle of eating light while traveling.

Misplaced Expectations - Namrata Mohan with her daughter, Ria Dutta, Age Eleven

Ria was struggling with her essay. When she shared it with me, I told her to substitute some words for better vocab and completely change the conclusion. Later I learned that she received an A without making any changes, "Mom you are a high school AP teacher and that's not how elementary school students write. So hold on to your misplaced expectations." I will never forget that my daughter has her voice and writing style that I should never bother changing.

Which Words Would sYou Believe - Namita Pandey with her son, Achintya, Age Seven

My family picked me up after my hair highlight appointment. Seeing my disappointment when they failed to notice the change, Aachu complimented, "Your hair looks beautiful." Then minutes later, when I denied stopping at the Yogurt Land, he retaliated with, "Your hair doesn't look nice. You wasted your money." Later at home, when he apologized, I told him that he had made it difficult for me to believe his words. His reaction stunned me: "Would you believe me when I am calm or when I am mad and say the opposite things." Now, I don't dwell on things my loved ones say when they are mad.

About the Authors

Our family bonds over philosophical conversations and tangible projects like CharityDress, a social enterprise, and this book. We live together in San Ramon, California. Nitya, a high schooler, strives to bring attention to complex issues shaping her generation through education, art, and debate. Naveli, a student at UC Davis, is pursuing her passion for psychology, women's studies, and dance to deepen our understanding of human behaviors. Manisha, their mom, led global roles at LinkedIn, eBay, and Oracle and endeavors to strengthen personal ties with awareness, accountability, trust, and technology.

Through their stories, they highlight the critical roles families play in shaping us with the hope of creating an even playing field for everyone to talk freely. So, when we talk, we won't have the superficial "how are you" and "I'm good" talks. Instead, we try to indulge in meaningful conversations to understand and strengthen each other. Continue the conversation at www.NaviNiti.com.

- Gunjan Garg (Dad)

Reviews

When We Talk, Let's Really Talk flows like a river. The surface is calm and familiar, and the depth takes the reader to a profound calm. The everyday slices of life blend beautifully with introspective insights by the three authors. The authors portray the complex interplay of mother-daughter-sibling relations by deconstructing rituals, intersectional identities, and challenges. The characters come alive because we know them. Using multiple family members' lenses is engaging - bringing in their unique perspectives as they try to understand each other and themselves.
- **Madhura Das Gupta, CEO, Aspire For Her, India https://www. aspireforher.org/**

I had many epiphanic moments as mum, daughter, sister, friend, and therapist while reading the stories of this incredible mother-daughters trio. By sharing how they found their conscious voice to communicate within themselves and each other, they also invite us to reflect on what is a *"real talk."* As circumstances can bias our relationships, this book illustrates how *love, awareness, curiosity,* and *respect* is a must for a nurturing family bond; thus, providing a breeding soil for our children implies welcoming them as equal individuals, with feelings, emotions, opinions and… a soul. A book for parents and educators because *"empowering begins at home."*
- **Sophie Roumeas – Hypnotherapist, holistic coach, and writer, France www.sophieroumeas.com**

The deep dives and multiple perspectives on family communication expanded my viewpoint on "effective communication." Naveli, Nitya, and Manisha invited me to their dining table and shared their openness, immersing me in their daily conversations. As a college student entering new phases of life soon, the importance of open communication to build my circle of trust will stick with me.
- **Shivani Amin, Dominican University of California, BSN Nursing, USA https://www.linkedin.com/in/shivani-amin/**

In *When We Talk, Let's Really Talk,* Nitya, Naveli, and Manisha take us on a personal journey that portrays the importance of positive discourse in forming our identities in a world where communicating is not a priority. As a high school student, this book reminded me of the importance of communicating with my loved ones in the authentic way Nitya, Naveli, and Manisha do. A must-read for everyone.

- Rani Vakharia, Student at Dougherty Valley High School, USA https://www.linkedin.com/in/rani-vakharia-2016371ba

When We Talk, Let's Really Talk... has been born out of pure tenacity to foster conversations among a mother and two daughters. As this compilation has taken place over several years that includes many difficult conversations full of heart-racing emotions, what is masterful is the fact that it has been documented, incised, and gives the reader over a hundred short sentences that describe the lessons learned. *The takeaway is unique and hard to find in the literary world.* A must for any family that wants to raise confident children with high self-esteem and a cohesive household. Bravo!!

- Shamshudin(Sam) Kherani, Chief Dental Officer, 123Dentist Corporation, Canada

An inspiring collection of life experiences of three women who have supported and learned from each other. A way of living where we don't just pass through life but live and learn from every experience. Their conversations make the book so very enjoyable! *Every reader will walk away with "something special."*

- Poonam Rana, Associate Director, National University of Singapore https://www.linkedin.com/in/ranapoonam/

When We Talk, Let's Really Talk is an honest reflection of how open conversations can simplify relationship equations. A gutsy compilation of deep thoughts, the book qualifies as a breezy read on the surface, but in hindsight, makes one introspect deeper into the dynamics they share within their families. Multiple vantage points to a binary situation make

it relatable and reassure that goofing up is alright and that lending an ear without judgment is the cornerstone of relationships.
- **Deepti Agrawal, founder www.deeptidesigns.com, USA**

As we stumble to find each other in this age of disconnection, *When We Talk, Let's Really Talk* demonstrates the transformational power of slowing down and exchanging stories within our families. In a time when attention spans are measured in mere seconds, Manisha, Naveli, and Nitya remind us that all humans desire to be seen, heard, and held. Within the complexities of our unique narratives and family dynamics lie the ability to discover our shared commonalities, be it in the fears we hold or the love we seek. *It is a fascinating and relatable read that inspires us to ask friends and family who they truly are and what they seek.*
- **Julia Harriet, USA https://juliaharriet.com/**

When We Talk, Let's Really Talk... beautifully weaves three different perspectives and experiences of mother, daughter, and sister into impactful, meaningful family conversations. Nurturing one another to become better versions of themselves, they share words that are sometimes difficult to say—*each favorite moment quickly replaced by another*. The book felt courageous, vulnerable, and honest - showing how to love and forgive by learning from one another.
- **Tiffani Jean Freckleton, RN. USA Author of *My NICU Story: Written with Love.***

Naveli summed this book up best when she wrote, '*Life had indeed started seeming like a bouquet of experiences.*' Told through the insights gained via their singular perspectives, this book conveys an overall sense that coming together, making the consistent effort to engage, communicate, and understand one another in a family unit is time well spent.
- **MacKenzie Nelson, USA, Author of *My Father's Feathers***

When We Talk, Let's Really Talk is a powerful and timely book about listening and establishing open dialogue with our children. The book shares

three perspectives of a mother and her two daughters, their experiences and feedback of the same events. This book is beautifully written and will inspire and lead you to have a more fulfilled connection and communication with your children. A gift to all parents.
- **Maureen Ryan Blake, Founder, Maureen Ryan Blake Media Productions, USA**

Open, honest, and authentic conversations shape both relationship building and perspective taking. It paves the way for understanding self and others to mindfully lead a family, organization, and society. *When We Talk, Let's Really Talk* provides realistic insights into how a family can intentionally cultivate a resiliently thriving future by developing inter-generational co-creative leadership!
- **Dr. Kasthuri Henry, PhD. CEO, KasHenry Inc & Founder, Ennobled for Success ™ Institute. www.kashenry.com**